HORSHAM'S HIDDEN HORRORS

by

S. J. SCARRY

PREFACE

Most of this book is historical and statistical fact drawn from local newspapers and books. The rest of the material (particularly some of the ghost stories) is hearsay and should be taken as such.

ACKNOWLEDGEMENTS

I would like to thank all those who took the time to share their stories and knowledge of local incidents with me. I would also like to thank West Sussex Libraries situated throughout the Horsham District for their excellent facilities and service.

FOR

George Wren and young Leney
Two undoubtedly innocent men who were executed at Horsham.

First published in Great Britain by S. J. Scarry
1996
3rd Edition 2004
ISBN 0 9520251 1 6

CONTENTS

HORSHAM'S GHOSTS

DISTRICT GHOSTS

DISTRICT HORRORS

HORSHAM HORRORS

HORSHAM'S GHOSTS

THE SPIRIT OF SQUIRE PAULLET

One well known local ghost was that of Squire Paullet. Seen mostly in St. Leonard's forest this apparition was said to enjoy jumping onto the back of your horse if you were ever foolish enough to travel through the wood after dark. Any attempt to communicate your displeasure at the Squire's antics was quite fruitless due to the fact that the ghost was completely headless!

Legend has it that the only way the mad Squire could be removed from one's back was by crossing the boundaries of the forest. This would cause the spectre to vanish into thin air.

How the Squire ever came to haunt St Leonard's forest is a mystery because his body (a certain Captain William Paullett of the Horse Grenadiers) lies buried in West Grinstead Church under a £2000 monument.

One explanation, maybe, is that smugglers made up the story in an attempt to scare people away from the woods whilst they carried out their illegal activities. This however does not account for the reportedly serious sighting of Paullett that took place besides one of the Hammer ponds in recent years. The story came from a woman who related that her husband had been in the forest and seen the headless figure beside one of the woodland waters. Other sources have mentioned that they heard a story concerning a woman driver who saw Paullett in Colgate. After stopping her car at a lay-by in Forest Road she apparently got out for something and saw the headless apparition in amongst the trees.

On another occasion in 1977, a group of teenage boys from a Horsham school were allowed to spend the night in the forest with a camera and trip wire in an effort to capture the restless spirit on film. During the night the weird noises they heard scared them so much they ran away leaving their equipment behind. It took them three days to summon up enough courage before returning for the abandoned gear.

THE SPECTRES OF THE CAUSEWAY

The road leading to St. Mary's Parish Church is possibly the oldest travelled route in the town.
It is not surprising then to learn that it is also haunted by a figure believed by some to be more than seven hundred years old.

There have apparently been several sightings of the spirit but the best and most reliable sighting was made by a Vicar resident in the 1940s. Late one evening the clergyman was doing his rounds and checking that all the doors were locked when, as he reached the north porch of the church, he had a strange feeling that he was no longer alone.

Looking around he noticed nothing at first but then he saw a dark shape that was moving up from the crypt. From here it began to resemble the shape of a man as it moved across the pathway to the entrance gates. It carried on up the Causeway and vanished into thin air as it walked by the Vicarage wall.

The Vicar describes the figure as being that of a monk because he was clearly wearing a habit and cowl. Horsham has never had a Monastery but it is written that John De Braose brought a brotherhood from the abbey of Fecamp in Normandy. These monks possibly frequented the crypt at St. Mary's leaving behind more than just their blessings.

A house situated halfway up the Causeway is also haunted by a strange unseen ghost. It seems to spend most of its time either on the stairs or in a room upstairs and makes its presence felt by lowering the immediate air temperature. The owner, who is quite unafraid of her resident spirit, even has a name for it.

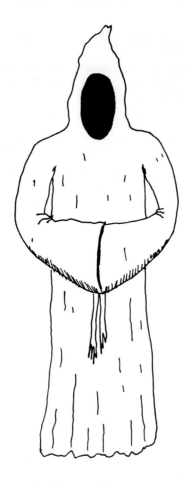

Fig. 1. The Phantom Monk emerges from the crypt of St. Mary's.

THE GHOSTS OF TOWER HILL

The house on the corner is reputedly haunted by the ghost of a Colonel or Major. If you pass by and look up at the top window he can sometimes be seen, in full uniform, looking out. The fact that the army was barracked at Tower Hill for many years seems to lend credence to this story.

A resident living further down the road in a small terrace house did at one time report that a certain downstairs room in the house was subject to unnaturally cold temperatures. He felt this may have been due to a ghostly presence that was seen at one time upstairs.
The occupier relays the story that he awoke one night to see a shadowy figure standing in the doorway of his bedroom. It is believed the ghost is that of a friend's granddad.

Another ghost said to haunt the area is that of a Drummer Boy. Some say that if you walk along the footpaths that run across the hill you stand a good chance of seeing him. The main path that runs from near the back of the Boars Head Public House is a well known fairy path and it's this fact that enables those who tread it to see strange things.

WHITEVANE POND, FOREST ROAD

Recently cleared of rhododendron bushes and enlarged, Whitevane pond is one of the biggest areas of water in the Horsham area. Stocked with large carp this basin is the headwater for the river Arun and attracts fishermen from all over the country.

But many people say there is more than just fish at Whitevane.

If, after arriving you decide to set up your gear on the left hand side of the back stretch, beware, because the locals know it as spook corner. In this area of the pond, immediately below the imposing old building of Forest Grange School, a ghost has been seen repeatedly walking along the banks under the great oak trees of the dark, forbidding forest.

The ghost or rather ghosts are said to be that of a woman and her dog. The woman has been described as having shoulder length light hair, a light coloured khaki type jacket and a longish dress. The dog type has not been identified.

One fisherman even reported hearing a girl's voice that cried, 'Get off me, leave me alone,' in the middle of the night. He believes the girl may have been attacked some time in the past or even murdered and that is why her spirit cannot rest.

All who have reported seeing the ghost say that it vanishes as it approaches the small overflow bridge situated below the Grange.

Another story says that builders who recently carried out work on the old Grange refused to work after dark because of certain 'strange things' that had happened.

THE GHOST OF THE HIDDEN POND

This body of water lies approximately one half mile directly north of Whitevane pond and the old Forest Grange School. At one time fished almost exclusively by the local constabulary some say this pond is haunted by a figure of a woman who appears in the mist that occasionally covers the water. Rumour has it that the reliability of the witnesses is beyond question as they themselves were actually both serving police officers.

But perhaps there is no such ghost, and the police, like the smugglers before them, have simply made up this story to keep curious folk away from their much prized fishing water. Although one would have thought this unlikely as the sight of an officer's uniform would surely be enough to scare anyone away from that part of the forest!

WHERE LIES THE SMUGGLERS POND?

Researches on black-marketeers show that a smuggler by the name of Pentecost drowned along with his packhorse in one of the forest ponds. This water is most likely to be Hawkins Pond as it was actually named after and probably frequented by the infamous bootleggers. But, unlike some of the other ponds, there doesn't seem to be any records of a ghost here (except possibly Paullett).

This may mean that Pentecost and his horse drowned elsewhere in the forest and that possible ghostly apparitions seen on other ponds may indeed be those of the sunken smuggler trying, along with his horse, to escape his watery grave. Perhaps, if he ever decides to unburden his horse of the smuggled goods it was carrying, the long dead pair may finally be able to manage an escape one of these dark, moonless nights.

Fig. 2. Is one of Horsham's ponds haunted by a drowned smuggler ?

THE SPIRIT OF ROOST HOLE

Legend has it that a man walking his dog along the edge this water somehow managed to fall in and drown. Some claim to have seen his spirit in the mist that frequently covers this low lying pond but others say that it appears in the form of a glow that seems to have its origins at the deepest part of the water.

Some modern fishing floats glow extremely brightly and it is just possible that people have seen one of these and mistaken it for something supernatural. This pond is known to be deep and so nobody, for safety's sake, should ever attempt to investigate any strange lights seen under the water.

Over the years many people have put forward theories and ideas concerning ghosts. The latest and probably best explanation for such apparitions has its foundation in electricity. Nowadays we think nothing of recording music and video on to tape cassettes. These plastic tapes are impregnated with iron so that when we send an electrical signal to them, (i.e., record on them) we actually change their magnetic signature and thus store our sound and vision. The current thinking points out that our bodies give out an electrical signal, (our aura) and that this could very well leave a recording of us on ground rich in iron. Our walking over a path is the exact opposite of a tape moving over a recording head but the end result is exactly the same.

Knowing as we do that water conducts electricity very well one might guess the best place to go looking for ghosts would be somewhere, A: saturated in iron ore, and, B; wet.

As the Hammerponds and Roost Hole were originally dug so that iron ore could be extracted from the ground this earth would seem to have the right credentials to store past images and events.

Or, as we prefer to call them, ghosts!

ST. JOHN'S CHURCH, HAMMERPOND ROAD

Of all the churches in Horsham, St Johns seems to have the most 'stories' attached to it. Standing as it does against the edge of a hurricane damaged forest the church itself looks altogether more welcoming than it did in years gone by. Before the storm huge trees towered up around the building giving it a dark and eerie backdrop. At night it was a place much feared by local youth and the last place you would want to pass on a cold, moonless night.

These youth never referred to the church by its proper name, preferring to call it Doomsday church instead. The front gate is an item much referred to in conversation as it appears to have been constructed like a five pointed star. Closer inspection reveals it to in fact be a six pointed affair that resembles the star of David.

SURGICAL SPIRIT

Several people have related this story of a doctor and his wife but no obvious proof seems to exist as to its authenticity.

It seems that way back in the mists of time a doctor and his good wife frequented the church at Doomsday regularly attending every Sunday service. And then something came between them that caused a serious and irreparable split in their marriage. It was then that the good doctor decided to do away with his troublesome partner. The story says that on one dark, still night he lured her on some pretence or other up the graveyard of the church and as clouds tumbled across a windy sky, strangled her to death amongst the headstones.

What he did with the body is not known but it is presumed that he buried her alongside the other unfortunate souls, it being the perfect place to hide a corpse.

To this day no one really knows if it ever happened at all, but one thing has convinced some that it did. Come the anniversary of the murder the smell of surgical spirit can be smelt wafting around the graveyard of this small, remote church.

TWO STROKE OR NOT TO STROKE

As was mentioned in the beginning, Doomsday church was not a place to linger after dark if you possessed an over active imagination. But for one youth, well aware of the stories surrounding the church, fate almost made his worst nightmare come true.

The individual in question travelled between Mannings Heath and Horsham on a regular basis. His preferred mode of transport was a two stroke motorcycle which was both economical and nippy to ride despite being fairly old.

On the night in question our motorcyclist was returning from Horsham along Hammerpond Road when he casually spied the church up ahead. Subconsciously his mind instructed his hand to open up the throttle of his machine a little more. He did not wish to spend more time than strictly necessary in the vicinity of the church.

As he drew level with the stone wall that surrounds the graveyard his engine cut dead and the bike began to coast. Though not a religious man we are told the biker began to pray most earnestly for his machine to start. But it was to no avail. Repeated opening of the throttle produced only the customary wallowing sound exhibited by two stoke engines in distress.

By now man and machine were directly opposite the church and the icy cold fingers of fear were beginning to get a real feel for biker leather. More feverish yanking of the throttle followed but the engine seemed well and truly dead. And still the bike rolled.

Slower and slower under a pitch black night sky.

Fully twelve yards from the end of the grounds the motorcyclist began to show real physical signs of the panic, until that moment, held securely within him. He most definitely did not want to break down here of all places.

Travelling barely one mile an hour the bike and rider passed the last corner of the stone wall and at the exact moment they did so the engine burst into life. And before you could say Jack Robinson the lucky biker disappeared into a cloud of blue/grey exhaust fumes.

To this day he swears it was the strange forces that did it. For the exact time he was opposite the church grounds his engine was as dead as a door nail. He says he was lucky to have entered the 'shadow' of the church at the speed he did. Any slower and he would never have escaped its grasp.

If any engine is likely to cut out in this way it would be a two stroke. The nature of their action means that lubricating oil is burnt with petrol making them dirty engines to run. This dirt often finds its way onto a plug causing it to cease functioning temporarily.

But it is still strange that it should choose to happen at the exact place it did. And even stranger that the problem should elect to clear itself when it did.

Coincidence?

Not if the biker has anything to say about it!

ALL IN A SPIN

The story goes like this. Three, or perhaps four, heavy metal music fans were either going to or returning from a gig. Travelling together in a car they found themselves on Hammerpond Road heading towards the church.
All except the driver were 'merry' or at least well on the way to being so when their car passed alongside Doomsday.

At this point some who tell the story say that the occupants of the car spoke amongst themselves of the church and its reputation. Being into heavy metal music they undoubtedly had some knowledge of things dark and perhaps referred to the church in this context.
If anything was said that night it makes little difference to what actually happened. Unless, that is, you believe firmly that certain forces detailed in the Bible actually have an influence over our lives.
For, on a night reportedly calm and dry, the car carrying the young men was, for a short time, possessed by a violent and yet exact force of unknown origin.
As it fell under the shadow of Doomsday the moving car was reportedly plucked from the ground, spun through a complete 360 degree arc and deposited back onto the road still moving.
One can only guess at the shock experienced by the occupants but if some of what people say is true it was pretty severe. The sceptics may say that the driver of the vehicle was also 'merry' and that this was the cause of the spin but those in the car swear that this was not the case. There was no screech of tyres during the spin and the steering wheel was not interfered with in anyway before the incident.
The section of road that passes the church is also straight meaning the driver would have had no cause whatsoever to turn the wheel.
Another coincidence?
Who really knows.
Only next time you have cause to fall under the shadow of the church on Doomsday Green, keep a tight grip on that steering wheel and do not, whatever you do, think of anything other than good thoughts!

THE GHOST OF THE BREWERY

Some of the buildings at the town's King and Barnes brewery are reputedly over one hundred years old and it is here that the ghost of Mr Williams is sometimes seen.
Mr Williams was once the head brewer on the site and he is reportedly seen on a regular basis still wearing the traditional white coat that is worn by all who have graduated to his high level. One sighting was by a Cellar-man who thought the ghost was actually a Customs Exciseman making a visit. He said good morning to the spirit only to see it turn and walk away. He later mentioned to a superior that he thought Customs were on site only to be told they were not. When he described the figure other employees immediately recognised it as Williams.
On another occasion five workers were in the fermentation room when a metal bucket full of water fell over of its own accord. Startled staff are reported to have left the room rather rapidly.

TOWN HALL SPIRITS

Workers do not like to work late in the Town Hall because they say it is haunted. Some have reported strange noises at night while others have seen ghostly things within the walls. The Hall was extensively altered in 1812 by the Duke of Norfolk but later pulled down in 1888 and rebuilt. The Hall today still stands on its original site so it is possible that some of the spectres may belong to condemned criminals who were once tried in the old building by the Horsham Assizes.

THE PHANTOM HITCH-HIKER

Many towns and places throughout the land have stories of phantom hitch-hikers connected with them and Horsham is no exception. A driver heading south on the London to Worthing Road is said to have stopped and offered a lift to a girl hitcher. The girl accepted the ride and the two set off. The driver found the girl to be very talkative and in their conversation the girl spoke of her family and home. As they drove through Horsham the driver pulled up at a cafe for a cup of tea but his passenger refused to leave the car to join him. The motorist left his companion, purchased a drink and returned to the car to find the girl had gone. Feeling worried for her the driver decided to ring her parents using information gleaned from her during their conversation.

On contacting her parents he discovered to his horror that the girl had in fact been killed three years earlier whilst trying to thumb a lift outside a Horsham cafe.

CHESWORTH'S GHOSTS

Chesworth is reportedly one of the most haunted places in Horsham though little detail about some of the hauntings actually exists. The site of the house itself is located three quarters of a mile to the south east of Horsham and is situated in a slight depression. In its day the manor house was surrounded by a moat but at the turn of the century this was only partly visible.

Evidence of what it must have been like in olden times came to light towards the end of the last century when the remains of the moat were cleared by the then tenant, Mr. Brooks. Along with things such as silt, weeds and general rubbish, a large quantity of human bones were dredged up from the bottom of the ditch. These presumably belonged to the soldiers of rival barons who from time to time felt it necessary to attack Chesworth.

One story speaks of blood stains that mysteriously appear within the manor on stonework, stains that cannot be removed no matter how hard people try.

Others tell of a ghostly presence that rings the bells unseen and lets forth ungodly shrieks. These screams are said to freeze the blood of any folk who hear them.

But the most fearful ghosts to encounter at this old country dwelling are those of the spectral riders. Being either ghosts of the original owner or indeed his enemies, these horsemen are said to appear in full battledress on a hill named Top Field that lies opposite the site of the house. At midnight they charge down at full gallop and in full cry.

Another story speaks of a family living on the estate and the legend that is connected with them. Their courtyard is part covered by wooded beams and it is with these that strange things happen. Whenever a member of the family dies another knot is said to mysteriously appear in one of the lengths of wood.

The most famous ghost of the area though seems to be that of Henry the eighth's executed wife, Anne Boleyn, who was at one time a frequent guest on the property. A ghost said to be that of her has been seen walking in one of the old courtyards thereabouts.

HORSHAM'S POLTERGEIST

Behind the old Catholic Church in Springfield Road was a house that was the scene of much poltergeist activity in the late 19th century. Some locals put the goings on at the time down to Richard Collyer, founder of Collyer's school. But the type of disturbances there were more likely to have been caused by a child or young person using the youth club based on the premises at the time.

In 1897, the parish priest, Father Munro, actually lived in the house in question and told fellow churchmen what he had experienced. He told of a crucifix that hung in the hall constantly falling to the floor and of loud footsteps in the unoccupied upstairs rooms. Sometimes the walls would sound as if someone were rapping on them, bells situated about the house would ring violently and the housekeepers dog would bristle and growl at unseen entities.

A friend of Munro's, Canon Langton George Vere, confirmed everything that was going on in the house and wrote it up in a fictionalised version which appeared under the heading 'The Clapper and the Bell', in 1897. One assumes the account given within this book is a fairly accurate representation of the events that took place at this residence.

After Father Munro told his story to the Duke of Norfolk, the Duke built a new presbytery for him on the opposite side of the road.

HAMPERS LANE HAUNTING

When a young woman's father passed away she, along with other relations, were required to help out on the family farm situated along Hampers Lane. One of the chores usually carried out by her father involved the feeding of the chickens. For this he would select a sack of feed and open it by pulling at the 'ripcord' stitched along the top. After removing this cord he had a habit of tying it into a figure of eight and hanging it on a nearby nail that protruded from the barn.

Whilst working alone one day the girl picked a sack to open and pulled at the cord but found it would not budge. After wondering for a moment about how to open the sack she settled on cutting it and retired to an old caravan to get a pair of scissors.

When she returned the bag had been opened and the cord, tied in a figure of eight, hung from the nail.

THE GHOST OF ROFFEY CORNER

The only details available on this ghost say that a cottage next to the cross-roads is the site of the haunting. In times past it was common to bury suicides at cross-roads so perhaps this is the poor soul of an unfortunate who couldn't bare life any longer. More probable is the theory that the poor person once lived in one of the cottages or perhaps was run over and killed at or near the cross-roads.

One other ghost haunts the Kings Road area but unfortunately very little information is available on the actual site or kind of haunting.

THE HAUNTING OF CAMBRIDGE ROAD

A house in Cambridge Road is haunted by one of the most active ghosts in the Horsham area. A man who once lived there tells of a spirit that used to enter a bedroom and sit at the end of his sister's bed. Downstairs, curtains would sometimes fly up in the air for no apparent reason and doors would open on their own when the ghost was at play in the lounge. Sometimes when a member of the family walked down the stairs they would hear footsteps directly behind them as if they were being followed. The most disturbing incident, though, occurred when those present in the lounge felt something come into the room. As they looked at the sofa the cushion suddenly became depressed as if someone had just sat on it.

Those that have visited the house say that you can feel the strange atmosphere as it chills your body.

THE KINGS ARMS

Reports say that when the Kings Arms had some work carried out on it builders found a child's shoe embedded in the wall. After this was removed all sorts of strange things began to happen.

It was custom in years gone by to bury or hide objects within the walls of houses to either settle or keep spirits at bay and it seems the removal of the shoe may have awoken a ghost or two.

It is interesting to note that when a builder found an old bottle and removed it from the wall of an old Pease Pottage cottage he began to feel as if he were not the only person on the property. He eventually pulled off the job saying he didn't like the atmosphere around the place.

DISTRICT GHOSTS

THE FOX INN, BUCKS GREEN

This 16th century pub is said to be haunted by a figure in a grey suit. After the Landlord had locked up the pub one night he sat down for a quiet drink with a friend only to see his companion turn as white as a sheet. He had apparently seen the figure by the window. Seconds later the curtains flew up into the air and hit the ceiling. The Landlord said at the time that there was no draft that could have caused the sudden movement.

Another strange thing happened when the owners removed an old nail from a wooden beam. They kept finding it placed back in the original hole. And on occasion the heavy door which is the main entrance to the pub has been seen to open, its latch lifted mysteriously by an unseen hand.

TUNING INTO THE FUTURE

An electronics engineer and his wife had a strange experience whilst in a car, near the Cheals Roundabout, on the A264 Horsham to Crawley road. As he drove the mini he suddenly heard over the radio that rock star Mark Bolan had been killed. He asked his wife if she'd heard the news report and she replied that she had. Fiddling with the radio he was unable to tune the weak signal in for further clarification. Frustrated, he checked out the television news and the papers on arriving home but was unable to find any mention of the singer songwriter at all.

Days later Mark Bolan died in a car crash.

THE GHOST OF BUCK-BARN CROSSROADS

In the month of October 1947, a young man name of Don Cottrell set off on his motorcycle to travel home to the village of West Grinstead, which is six miles south of Horsham. It was a cold and frosty night and the biker was concerned enough to go carefully. Slowing down as he drew near to the Buck Barn cross-roads he was quite astonished to see an old man, raggedly clad, sitting on the milestone just off to his right. Before he could fully stop, the figure rose up and glided, its feet being some way from the ground, out into his path.

Unable to even think about taking avoiding action due to the suddenness of the old man's actions he ran down the figure and experienced a sudden chill that was quite unearthly in its intensity. Braking hard he stopped his machine and ran back to the site of the collision to help the old man he felt sure he had injured only to find nothing but an empty road. Stunned and not a little panicked he jumped back onto his machine, gunned the engine and set off for home at breakneck speed.

On telling his family of the ghostly encounter his father insisted on returning to the spot that very night to make sure no one lay injured or dying. After his arrival he searched high and low but found nothing but a quiet road and a freezing wind.

20 Years later the family heard that the story of the ghost at Buck Barn cross-roads had actually been told by others on the BBC's Woman's Hour programme proving that many people had seen the old man.

In recent years the road has been widened into a dual carriageway and it seems this may have had the effect of banishing the ghost as no further reports of sightings have come to light.

COWFOLD MONASTERY

During the war Soldiers were billeted at Cowfold Monastery and it was not long before they realised they might have an unseen adversary in their midst. The first indications that something was amiss came when soldiers on sentry duty began avoiding a certain cloister for unspecified reasons. When someone tried to walk through that particular cloister with several Alsatian guard dogs the animals began to growl and raise their hackles without good reason.

All concerned came to the conclusion that the cloister was home to a ghost of some sort although no witness has ever seen any visible signs of a spirit.

SOUTHWATER GHOST

One lady tells of her Grandfather who believed his barn was haunted. Every night he would return at 9.00pm to 'rack the horses' and if he found them in an agitated state he would blame it on the ghost of the stables. Some people say that fairies are responsible if horses are found disturbed and sweating.

HEADLESS IN HENFIELD

With many smugglers passing through this little village in years gone by it is not surprising that stories have come into being concerning local woods. These desperate men would deliberately spread scary stories in an effort to rid the immediate area of inquisitive people.

One story possibly made up by the smugglers tells of a large, ghostly animal about half the size of a calf. With fiery red eyes this animal is said to stalk a small forest in the area looking for victims to gorge on. Another tale tells of a headless woman who sits on Pickwell Bridge, spinning wool.

KNEPP CASTLE

This old ruin situated by the side of the Horsham to Worthing Road is supposedly haunted by the ghost of a white doe said to be the spirit of a young girl who fell victim to witches' curses in the 13th century. Referred to as Cnap Castle in early documents this structure is believed to have been built shortly after the Norman Conquest.

THE HAUNTING OF TILLETTS LANE, WARNHAM

Anyone venturing into Tilletts Lane after dark should beware. It is said by many local folk that the top end is haunted by a ghost of a hanging man. The majority say it is that of a farmer named Tillett who hanged himself from one of the forest trees along the lane. One local woman remembers that her mother used to warn her not to stay out too late telling her that the ghost of Old Tillett might get her.

RUSPER GHOSTS

The Star Public House in Rusper is said to be haunted by the ghost of a drinker. On some nights the murky figure of the spook can be seen sitting on a stool in front of the main bar. On other nights he has been known to turn all the beer pumps off and put the lights out.

THE GHOST OF BROADBRIDGE HEATH LANE

Anyone contemplating a midnight walk along the lane from Broadbridge Heath to Warnham should seriously think about taking the car according to local residents. Legend has it that the screams of the last person burned to death on Broadbridge Heath Common can sometimes be heard along this dark and enclosed byway late at night.

Found guilty of murder and sentenced to be fired in August, 1752, Ann Whale, a single mother, was executed on the village Common before a large crowd.

For further information see:- BURNED AT THE STAKE IN HORSHAM.

RUDGWICK GHOSTS

Some folk say that the Kings Head Public House in Rudgwick is haunted by a ghost that is fond of cleaning the rooms in that old building. In the dead of night a duster can at times be heard brushing over the furniture in a vain effort to clear it of dirt. The ghost has never been seen but apparently also likes to lift certain latches up occasionally.

One ghost that most definitely has been seen is 'The Lady in Grey'. She is said to have haunted the old manor house at Baynards Park until it was burnt down. Legend has it that she was a servant girl who fell in love with a Gamekeeper on the estate. He began to visit her at night but was caught in the act and beheaded on the balcony. The servant girl standing below caught his head in her apron and from that day on her spirit has wandered the grounds in sorrow.

She was seen once by two cleaners as she rose, clothed in a dark cape and hood, from a big old oak chair to float into a nearby bedroom. On another occasion a housekeeper saw her at dusk on the long drive that leads to the house. All witnesses say that they felt no fear at all, only peace. They also spoke of a strange and glowing kind of light that appeared to emanate from the young girl's ghost.

Others say that when Sir Thomas More was executed by Henry VIII, his daughter brought his head back to the family home and kept it for many years in an old wooden chest.

One further strange story told of heavy knocks that sometimes emanated from the manor house stair case while it was in existence. Some said it sounded as if something round and weighty were rolling slowly down the steps. No object was ever seen to be making these noises but those who heard them believed the sound was made by a ghostly severed head.

THE GHOSTLY MONKS OF FURNACE LAKE

Just off the A 281 Guildford Road lie Furnace Ponds. Situated at the edge of Roman Woods, these two bodies of water stretch out north west away from Furnace house. By far the largest of the ponds is the second one which must be in the region of several hundreds of yards long.

At the end of this water there lies on the right hand side a small feeder stream that runs down from the forest. And it is from here that the ghostly monks are said to appear.

Forded by a narrow iron footbridge the feeder stream is itself bordered by an overgrown footpath that leads back in the direction of several local farms. Whilst fishing on the back stretch of the lake many anglers have reported seeing these spectral figures emerge from the trees and float down to the water's edge apparently in search of fish. It seems that this water, described as 'Pond Bay' on the Ordnance Survey map, was once used by local monks who bred carp amongst others to eat.

Actual evidence that these monks existed is thin on the ground but some of the properties over the back of Roman Woods have distinctly religious sounding names in Bury St Austen's and Monks Farm. This suggests that reported sightings of robed figures hovering around the great lake may not be something to be laughed at.

In another incident a fisherman caught a 19 pound fish in the smaller of the two ponds and was approached by a man who congratulated him on his catch. The fisherman asked the stranger if he would take a photograph of the creature and turned around to pick up his camera. When he turned back the man had disappeared into thin air!

THE ADVERSANE SAILOR

The lane stretching between Adversane and Broadford Bridge is said to be the sight of a nautical haunting. In days gone by a sailor is said to have visited the local village pub, The Blacksmith's Arms, and boasted of how much money he carried. After a heavy night of drinking he set off along the lane and was set upon by robbers and murdered. To this day some say his ghost can still be seen on a certain section of this winding road.

Another haunted site in Adversane was the area where The Shepherd's Oak once stood. The shepherd is said to have been murdered here after winning some prize money at a local fair. In later years the tree was struck and destroyed by lightning.

GHOSTLY MONK OF LOXWOOD

Many people in Loxwood believe that the hooded figure sometimes seen near a certain accident black spot is either that of a monk from the old monastery at Drungewick Manor or the former owner of that estate. The ghostly figure is said to just stand and stare into space.

THE HAUNTED POOL AT POYNINGS

In 1883, a terrible tragedy occurred at Poynings when two small boys drowned in one of the two village ponds. A third boy, seeing his friends were in desperate trouble, ran to the nearby church to raise the alarm but he was too late.

To this day it is said that the ghost of the third child can still be seen as he runs in vain from the pond to the place of worship.

THE DANCING SKELETONS OF BROADWATER

Surely one of the most terrifying sights ever to have been seen must have been the Dancing Skeletons of Broadwater. Lying just north of Worthing, Broadwater is nowadays a quiet town suburb but if the writings of a certain Mrs Latham are anything to go by things get a little more lively around Midsummer's Eve.

In the late nineteenth century she wrote:

'There stood, and may still stand, upon the Downs close to Broadwater, an old oak tree that I used, in days gone by, to gaze at with an uncomfortable and suspicious look, from having heard that always on Midsummer's Eve, just at midnight, a number of skeletons started up from its roots, and, joining hands, danced around it till cock-crow, then as suddenly sank down again. My informant knew several persons who had actually seen this dance of death, but one young man in particular was named to me, who, having been detained by business at Findon till very late, and forgetting that it was Midsummer's Eve, had been frightened (no very difficult matter, we may suspect) out of his very senses by seeing the dead men caper to the rattling of their own bones.'

THE DITCHLING GHOSTS

South east of Ditchling lies Black Dog Hill. The road that runs past here to Westmeston is said to be haunted by a ghostly dog the likes of which are quite common in Sussex folklore. Other strange spirits can be listened to up on the nearby Ditchling Beacon. Some say that a ghostly hunt can sometimes be heard in all its glory as it thunders by unseen. The sound of the dogs, the horses hooves and the huntsman's horn can all be experienced by anyone unlucky enough to cross the path of the pack.

Let us hope that the fox was as invisible to them in their day as they are to us in ours!

CHANCTONBURY RING

This ancient ring of trees high up on the Downs has several stories connected with it. One says that if you walk around the trees twelve times on Midsummer's Eve an old Druid will rise up out of the earth and come to you. Another twist on the twelve times around the trees theme says that if you do the walk backwards (some feat!) the Devil will appear to you. Others say that this will conjure up Caesar who will again command his legions to conquer all England.

In 1935 a doctor and his wife were out walking when they apparently came upon a very scary scene amongst the trees. They would tell no-one what they experienced. Later in 1967, a group of students fled the site leaving valuable recording equipment behind. They too would not speak of what had happened to them.

Other stories tell of strange things that happened to U.F.O. spotters who dared venture into the trees after dark. Reports say that they were lifted from the ground and thrown about like rag dolls by an unknown force. Some felt their arms and legs seize up completely.

The ring is now a shadow of its former self due to the destruction caused by the recent hurricane.

THE HIGHWAYMAN OF CISSBURY RING

When a Highwayman was hanged near the Ring, it is said that he swore he would never 'sleep' in his grave. His body was taken down and laid to rest along one of the wide mud tracks that served as roads. But the next morning it was found to be lying on top of the grave.

From that time on travellers began to report sightings of the deceased robber saying his body appeared on the road before them. Some even said they heard a noise as their carriage rolled over the ghostly thief.

DISTRICT HORRORS

SUSSEX WEATHER, STORMS AND EARTHQUAKES

1158: Earthquake in Sussex killed three people in the west. The east was hit harder. 30 died.

1247: 11 churches in East Sussex destroyed by earthquake. There were 50 casualties.

1382: Earthquake. Many buildings damaged in Sussex.

6th April, 1580: Earthquake rings the bell in Chichester Cathedral. This quake was mentioned in Shakespeare's Romeo and Juliet.

3rd June, 1747: An extremely violent thunderstorm hits Midhurst and resulting rainwater destroys a bridge.

1750: Many earthquakes felt in Sussex over a period of three months. Many people began to think that the end of the world was nigh!

1st November, 1755: Lisbon earthquake felt in Sussex. Fish were left high and dry at Midhurst after water was hurled several feet from ponds.

June, 1791: Snow on the Downs in midsummer.

29th July, 1816: A violent whirlwind / waterspout seen at Arundel stretching up into the clouds.

20th January, 1838: Temperatures drop to -26.7C at Horsham. Anybody who felt a drink might warm them up was out of luck. Bottled gin froze solid.

11th July, 1888: Known as the year of no summer. Snow fell on the village of Rusper this day.

RUSPER CURSE

A gypsy woman put a curse on three magistrates as she was led from court in 1982. She had been illegally parked in one of the village lanes and was ordered to move on.

OLD SUSSEX REMEDIES

With many people unable to afford proper medical treatment in olden times it is not surprising that many turned to the so called alternatives. Some felt that rheumatism was best kept at bay by carrying a dead man's bone around on their person whilst others believed that an odd shaped stone or potato would suffice. One man even swore that he was cured of bad joints after friends buried him up to his neck one night in a local churchyard. After being dug up two hours later he said he felt completely cured.
 If you went down with whooping cough you were most likely to be prescribed baked mice and onions. But if you were lucky enough to be just a bed-wetter you would have been given jam with your mouse. Those looking a little jaundiced probably looked more so after their medicine. They were asked to swallow a live spider wrapped in butter.

RUSPER HOG

In 1793, a wild hog which stood more than 12 hands (four feet) high was killed at Rusper. The animal was measured at 9ft 6inches long and weighed in at an incredible 116 stone 6lbs. Imagine going for a quiet walk in the countryside and running into this beast. With jaws powerful enough to chew through bone these pigs were something to be feared.

Fig. 3. A giant Hog attacks two men at Rusper, 1793.

ALL SAINTS CHURCH, ROFFEY

The workers who built the All Saints Church at Roffey in 1878 were horrified when a white swan crashed into one of their scaffold poles and fell to the ground dead. But Mrs Cecil Martyn, who had built the church as a memorial to her dead husband, took the incident to be a good omen. The family crest was, after all, a white swan!

RUSPER'S SCROOGE

When the artist Hogarth began to paint The Miser's Feast he wondered who he could base the main character on. It wasn't long before he had decided that Rusper's very own Sir Isaac Shard should serve as the perfect model. Sir Isaac had a reputation equal to none when it came to being careful with money. But as the painting progressed Hogarth must have confided in one person too many as the secret soon got back to the Shard household. One day, as the master continued working in his studio, Sir Isaac's son burst in, drew his sword and slashed a hole in the middle of the picture!

THE SUSSEX PUMA

When hunter John Elliott went out after rabbits in October, 1990, he got more than he bargained for. As he crept through the woods at the end of Parish Lane, Pease Pottage, he stumbled upon a small group of five deer. Almost immediately he realised he wasn't the only one to have seen them for between them and him crouched a giant cat.

Elliott said later that, 'It was a jet black cat, as big as a large Alsatian, with a two foot tail. I don't mind admitting I was frightened. I think it was a puma. It was stalking the deer.'

A police spokesman said at the time: 'If you see the animal stand very still. Don't run away or it might treat you as prey. Do not approach it. We haven't been able to find any remains of its prey. It may just be a big dog but we are keeping an open mind on the matter.'

Over the years there have been many sightings of big cats around Sussex. Reports have come in from Arlington, Ringmer, Seaford, Ashurstwood, Lewes, Woodingdean, Horn, near East Grinstead, Storrington and Plumpton.

THE MONKS GATE MURDER

Monks Gate became the scene of a murder in 1776 when a man named Lindfield killed another by the name of Naldrett. At 6.00am on the morning of the 14th of October, Lindfield went to Monks Gate Toll House and called out to the young girl who lived there with her mother. Linfield was in love with the young girl, who was crippled, and when the mother asked what he wanted Linfield said he wanted to shoot her daughter.

The old woman started screaming and this brought Naldrett running to her assistance. Lindfield saw the other man as a rival in love and did away with him on the spot by shooting him.

Lindfield was arrested and found guilty but insane. He was sentenced to be detained at His Majesty's pleasure.

THE DOG EATERS OF PETWORTH

In 1760, the 'London Evening Post' reported an incident which had happened at the Half-Way Bridge Public House near Petworth. The episode began when a man and his hound entered the Inn. A local drinker, one of a party of four, accidentally injured the man's Newfoundland dog causing its owner to complain. One of the group then told the animal's keeper to pipe down, otherwise they would eat his dog.

It seems that after this statement was made certain wagers were effected between all concerned which resulted in the poor dog (named Caesar) finding his way onto the main course. The four men then ate the animal and apparently won half a guinea's worth of drink from the Landlord.

THE ITCHINGFIELD SKULL

When builders began restoration work on the Church in 1865, they found something that both surprised and scared them. Sitting on a roof beam and looking directly in their direction was a grinning skull. Many people have put forward views as to who owned the head, some saying that it belonged to Sir Hector Maclean, a man who believed in and fought for the Young Pretender in 1715. He apparently once hid himself away in the church fearing his life was at risk.

Another story about the Church suggests that if you search hard enough around it you will be rewarded by the sight of a bullet hole. My source does not say who made it but perhaps that is a question best left unasked.

THE ALFOLD DENE BELL

A commonly told story from the Rudgwick area concerns the whereabouts of a large bell said to have been cast in Rome. Various versions of the story exist but all say it fell from a wagon whilst being transported by the Roman Gate area. This site was apparently very swampy in days gone by and the big bell is said to have sunk almost straight away.

After failing to locate the bell several of the men went to a local witch who told them that if they ever wanted to see it again they should take 12 white oxen to the spot one midnight and throw a chain into the bog. As they left her cottage she warned them that if anyone of them spoke during the operation the bell would again be lost. The men did as they were told and managed to get a hook on the bell but, just as it broke the surface of the swamp someone said, 'We've got the Alfold Dene gurt Bell, in spite of all the devils in hell'. And at that moment the chain broke and the bell sunk never to be seen again.

ROAD CRASH AT HANDSCROSS

England suffered its first serious road accident in June, 1906, when an omnibus Vanguard crashed against a large oak tree near the village of Handscross. A party of Firemen from St. Mary's Cray and Orpington were on the bus for a day out in Brighton when the brakes failed at the top of a hill near to the Red Lion Public House. The speed of the bus increased from 12 mph until the driver could no longer control it. The vehicle hit the tree killing eight people instantly. The impact was such that many of the passengers were catapulted into the branches of the tree. A ninth traveller died two hours later while a tenth lasted a further two days.

The inquest was opened in the Red Lion but speaker had to keep their voices down as some of the injured and dying were being cared for in the next room. The final verdict which came in August found no one criminally responsible for the accident. A disaster fund set up for the victims and their families raised £3000.

HORSHAM HORRORS

HORSHAM HIT BY EARTHQUAKES!

At 8.30pm on Sunday March 31st, 1883, Horsham was rocked by an earthquake. People ran from their houses as pictures rattled on walls, House-bells started ringing and weighing scales moved as the earth did.
No major damage was done by the quake and no after shocks felt.

An earlier account of an earthquake was recorded by John Baker. On the 6th of January, 1772, he mentions in his diary of having experienced a tremor. At the time he was living in Horsham Park House.

UFOs OVER HORSHAM

North of Roffey lies Channells (older books say Chennells) Brook, Bush Lane and Castle Copse. If one proceeds down Bush Lane from Rusper Road you will soon find a small copse of trees on your left. It was here that during the late seventies / early eighties a large flying saucer was sighted by two youths.
At approximately midday the two teenagers walked their dogs down from the Lambs Farm estate, over the railway stile and on to the area of the copse. Whilst in these woods a great disk apparently came down until it was just above the tree tops and hovered for sometime.
The two youths and their panic stricken pets ran back to their estate as fast as their legs would carry them. The incident was never reported by the boys to the authorities for fear that they may not be believed. Both witnesses wish to remain anonymous.
Midway though the eighties a crop circle appeared in a corn field not 500 yards away from the area of the sighting and was photographed for the local paper.

In later years many people around Horsham, Southwater and Partridge Green reported seeing a U.F.O. like object over several days. A fireworks display at Knepp Castle was thought by some to be the cause of the strange lights but one witness described an object bigger than a plane with a white light shining down from its underside. Another witness who worked at a Space Science Laboratory said, ' I saw the fireworks display and it wasn't that.'

GREAT STORMS OF THE PAST

On Tuesday, the 29th of November, 1836, Horsham was hit by a tremendous storm that, much like the recent hurricane, tore down trees and buildings. The streets were reportedly full of thousands of broken slates and many chimney stacks whilst around ten trees in Springfield Park were blown down across North Parade.
Mick Miles Race was also hit badly losing many fully mature trees to the wind. Further reports say the town suffered extremely cold weather in 1838 and was hit by another bad storm in 1843.

September the 5th, 1958, saw Southwater hit by hail stones that measured three inches by one. These reportedly smashed green-houses to bits as they fell from the sky in their many thousands. In Pulborough, at the Codmere Hill nurseries, 13,000 panes of glass were broken. A woman worker said that the noise made sounded like machine gun fire. Soon after the stones came a whirlwind that ripped the roof from the recently rebuilt Southwater Garage and deposited it approximately a quarter of a mile away. Many farmers in the area lost all of their harvest and a large oak tree situated at the corner of Horsham Football Field was snapped in two approximately four feet from the ground. This fact alone is quite amazing when the trunk itself was three feet thick!

Between the 14th and 16th of September, 1968, north West Sussex was hit by some of the worst flooding it had ever seen. As Billingshurst was cut off completely and a man in Bucks Green was forced to seek refuge in a tree, Warnham Mill Pond swelled to such a level that the sluice gates had to be opened incase they broke under the waters weight. The resulting wave swept down Red River and caused the Arun to rise to a height 10 feet above normal. This gave rise to severe flooding in the Blackbridge Lane area.

The events of the 16th of October, 1987, will not be forgotten in a hurry by any resident of Horsham. The hurricane that formed over the English Channel early that winter's morning caused fearsome damage to a large part of the south east destroying countless buildings and trees. Many awoke to find dustbins, porches and even satellite dishes had been whisked away never to be seen again. Many workers from around the country were brought in to help with the clean-up.

EAGLES THAT DIED AT HORSHAM

There was no such thing as conservation in the Horsham of 1798. If there had been someone would surely have been charged after they brought down an eagle in the town that had a wingspan of 7 feet 3 inches. The bird stood 30 inches high. Sources record that a second bird was killed sometime in 1803. This had a wingspan of 8 feet. On the 11th of January, 1804, another was killed, also measuring 8 feet from wing tip to wing tip. This bird was shot by a miller named Tobitt on Horsham Common.
These last two birds may actually have been one and the same but the dates and sources seem to be reliable.

CIVIL WAR IN HORSHAM

Horsham saw very little action during the Civil War but it is reported that a group of Parliamentarians entered the town at one stage and clashed with the Royalists. The King's men apparently put up a good fight and forced their enemies from the streets of the town to take refuge in the surrounding countryside. Here the fighting continued for some hours with the guns being fired almost continually until the affair ended.
The numbers of wounded were not recorded but we do know that one soldier and three of the town's inhabitants lost their lives. The three townsfolk are listed in the Parish Register as:- Edward Filder, killed by soldiers who thrust a sword through the window of his house in the back lane, William Baker, killed in the hop gardens belonging to Nicholas Sturt, and Thomas Marshall, Gent, who was followed into east Street and killed near Thomas Michell's door.
The identity of the soldier that died is not known but it is thought that it could be John Michell, of Stammerham. Family records show he lost his life in an engagement with the Cromwellians at Horsham in 1648. His son was wounded in the same battle.

WORLD WAR TWO

The town of Horsham suffered some damage during the war caused by German bombs and crashing planes.
Some bomb drop sites were as follows:-

1940:

23rd, September: Around 100 incendiary bombs dropped east of Rusper house.

25th/26th, September: U.X.B. Kerves Lane. 2 H.E. (high explosive) bomb craters at Cowfold, 1 U.X.B.

1st, October: Chennells Brook, Roffey hit by 4 H.E. bombs. Little Haven Crossing Hit By 3 H.E. bombs. One Bungalow damaged.

3rd, October: Two bombs dropped at Steyning killed a number of cattle. 2 H.E. and 2 Oil bombs dropped at Hawkins Pond.

6th, October: German bomber dropped a charge onto railway lines just the other side of Worthing Road Bridge. A goods train carrying an urgent load packed into sixteen wagons and destined for Portsmouth crashed into the crater. The train driver, Tom Brackpool, and his fireman escaped injury.

11th, October: 4 H.E. bombs dropped at Southwater. Railway line blocked.

18th, October: 2 cottages in Lower Beeding slightly damaged by 2 H.E. and 1 Oil bomb. Cowfold hit by 2 H.E.s. No one hurt.

26th, October: Railway line at Southwater blocked by 1 H.E.

27th, October: 2 H.E.s dropped on Lower Beeding. No one hurt.

31st, October: 2 H.E. bombs dropped at Mannings Heath. No one hurt and no damage done.

29th, November: Eight houses destroyed and ten others severely damaged after three H.E. bombs fell on Orchard Street. Seven people lost their lives and ten were seriously injured.

1941:

12th, January: Incendiary bombs fall in Horsham Urban District.

11th, June: Single bomb dropped but it failed to explode.

1943:

10th, February: Four H.E. bombs fell on Wimblehurst-Richmond Road area causing two houses to be demolished and seven seriously damaged. Three people were severely injured.

20th, November: One H.E. bomb fell in a garden in Guildford Road. Three houses were seriously damaged.

1944:

24th, March: Many incendiary bombs fell near Pondtail Road causing two ricks to be set on fire.

29th, June: V.1. flying bomb shot down over Christs Hospital.

21st, July: V.1. exploded near Chesworth Farm. Buildings at Chesworth, Denne Road, Queen Street and Brighton Road damaged.

1945:

26th, January: Report issued in Crawley says 1,100 houses have been damaged by bombs since the previous June.

The following are some of the planes that were shot down or crashed in the Horsham area during the war years :-

1940:

21st, April: Hurricane crashed at Cowfold.

18th, August: German plane brought down at Steyning. Two crew died later from their injuries.

30th, August: Heinkel He 111H-2, shot down and crashed at Mannings Heath at 11.30am.

4th, September: German fighter brought down at Steyning.

9th, September: Junkers 88a-1 shot down by 66 sq and crashed at Newells Farm, Nuthurst. 2 Germans unhurt, 2 wounded.

9th, September: Messerschmitt Bf 109e-4, shot down by T.A.Vigors and crashed at Roman Gate, Slinfold. Pilot baled out.

9th, September: Spitfire crashed at Loxwood. Plane was a complete wreck.

1st, October: Spitfire crashed at Henfield.

29th, October: Messerschmitt Bf 109e-1, shot down and crashed in flames at Plummers Plain. Pilot Unteroffizier Alfred Lenz was rescued but died from his burns.

29th, October: Heinkel He 111H-2, rammed by Hurricane and crashed at Swires Farm, Capel.

1941:

13th, February: Beaufighter crashed at Needs Farm, Partridge Green. No one was hurt.

12th, March: Heinkel 111 shot down at Ockley. Only surviving crew member, Karl Brunning, treated at Horsham Hospital.

13th, March: Bomber shot down in flames (probably same plane as that mentioned on 12th). German pilot found in a field at Pondtail Road, his chute unopened.

14th, March: Heinkel 111 crashed at Smokehouse Farm, Shipley. Four crew buried at Hill's Road Cemetery.

17th, April: Junkers 88, crashed at Slaughter Bridge, Guildford Road. Crew buried at Hill's Cemetery.

27th, August: Hurricane crashed at Holbrook night affiliation flight with a 'Turbinlite' Havoc. Pilot Sgt. E. Bloor killed after his chute apparently failed.

27/28th, July: Junkers 88 shot down at Partridge Green damaging houses. All four crew died. It is said a large black rubber skid mark can still be seen on the end wall of a house. This was caused by one of the plane's wheels.

1942:

2nd, October: Spitfire makes a forced landing at Partridge Green after running out of fuel.

1943:

6th, June: 2 Spitfires collided over Horsham crashing at Spurs Orchard, Forest Road and at unknown site near Colgate. One pilot survived, one died.

13th, August: Lancaster bomber crashed at Wild Barkford, Plaistow, Loxwood.

20th, November: Focke Wulf 190, exploded in field near Wickhurst Lane, Broadbridge Heath. Pilot, Feldwebel Kurt Jorga parachuted into Cobb's Wood, Billingshurst and was taken prisoner.

6th, December: 2 Spitfires collide over Horsham. One crashed somewhere near Colgate the other at Spurs Orchard, Forest Road. One pilot survived.

1944:

19th, April: Messerschmitt 410a-1, shot down by Mosquito and crashed at Cooks Farm, Nuthurst. 2 crew killed.

25th, May: Spitfire crashed at Maplehurst. Ammunition exploded but pilot survived.

8th, June: 2 Mitchell bombers collided over Horsham and crashed at east side of Picts Hill, Worthing Road and a field near Kerves Lane. In all 8 air crew died.

3rd, August: Spitfire crashed at Billingshurst. Pilot badly injured.

Other notable incidents:-

A man cycling down Mill Lane, near to the Crabtree Public House was targeted by a German fighter plane (probably a Messerschmitt of Focke Wulf) which dived at him. As it opened up with its machine guns and raked the small road with bullets the cyclist was forced to dive from his machine into a ditch. The man incurred no injuries from the attack.

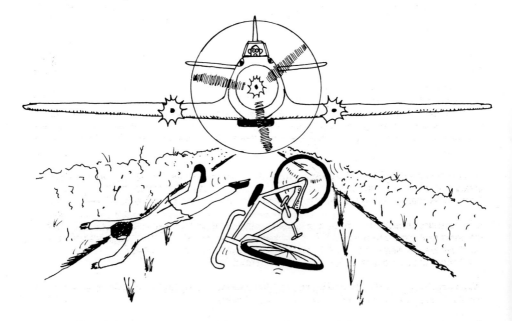

Fig. 4. A German fighter machine guns a local man during World War II.

It is not widely known that prisoners of war were kept behind high wire fences near St. Johns Church, Hammerpond Road. Some townsfolk remember seeing them as they walked down Sun Oak Road, and described them as being possibly from an area known as White Russia. Others in the area believed them to be 'White Poles'. The prisoners were known locally for carving toy chickens and men out of wood. Some would show passers-by pictures of their families and children. When news came through that these men were to be repatriated one prisoner in the Mannings Heath area is said to have dressed himself carefully in his best uniform and then hanged himself.

William Joyce, the infamous Lord Haw-Haw, once lived at West Chiltington. During one of his notorious broadcasts he stated that: ' We have not forgotten Steyning.'

Through the war, ambulance drivers slept in the Ritz Cinema so they could easily get to the nearby garage if they were needed in an emergency. One night two soldiers, armed with guns, broke in to the building to rob the till. The night watchman was tied up along with cleaners as they arrived for work but the Manager, a Mr.Ellison, never arrived to open the cash register and the men fled empty handed. Later that morning troops and police surrounded the building in the hope of catching the men but they had long since gone.

Two boys were treated for hand and facial injuries after a bomb detonator exploded in their hands.

One report says that an empty house owned by the Mills Family was destroyed by a 'Doodlebug'. The property was situated south-east of Leonardslee. Some say a V1 may have come down in the Barns Green area.

During the war the local paper reported on several incidents involving Canadian soldiers. One man shot himself accidentally whilst out hunting rabbits and another, a despatch rider, was killed speeding. A Horsham man was killed in another incident when a soldier's motorcycle hit a cyclist, a pedestrian and a parked car. A Horsham motorcyclist was killed in Kerves Lane by a Canadian lorry travelling on the wrong side of the road.

Crashed German aircraft were put on display in Horsham to help raise morale and funds for the town Spitfire.

An Allied Ammunition Dump was set-up at Crabtree during the war. The bombs and bullets stored there were only ever moved during the night. In the late '70s schoolboys from the area recovered seven live tracer bullets from a pond. Six were copper jacketed while the seventh was a hollow tipped Dum Dum. They also removed gunpowder from an old shell case and buried the explosive in a field. Several months later the boys had cause to go back to the area and found a large crater where they had left the shell's propellant.

An Officer in the R.A.F. was charged with the murder of his wife on the 16th of May, 1941. The doctor stated that there were many bullet holes in the woman's body. Later that year, on the 11th of July, a woman was charged locally with attempted murder after she hit her sleeping husband with an axe.

One Horsham woman tells of being in her garden and hearing a V1's engine cut out. She dived onto the grass expecting to hear a loud blast but heard absolutely nothing. Did this bomb land locally and was it recovered? May it still be out there somewhere buried in an isolated wood?
 Next time you go for a quiet walk in the country, tread carefully!

When Lord Woolton visited Horsham and asked the townsfolk if they had any complaints someone told him the local police had been acting like the German Gestapo!

Bombs dropped by an FW190 at Steyning killed an old woman and her dog and destroyed terraced houses opposite Chantry Green. In another incident at the village a Dornier flew low over the houses and machine gunned a wall. No one was injured.

A Heinkel crashed in Hammer Pond Woods. The aircraft appeared to be complete as it entered the trees but it blew up on impact. A witness described how a piece of shrapnel or wreckage flew over his head seconds after the explosion.

War games were conducted around Mannings Heath during the war. Canadian Soldiers, dressed in full German uniform, attacked the village and tried to capture several local pill boxes.

During the war the people of Horsham raised enough money (£5000) to enable a fighter to be built on the town's behalf. On the 9th of January, 1942, the West Sussex County Times printed a picture of Horsham's Spitfire under the headline, 'Now On Service!'
Unfortunately the plane had been at the bottom of the English Channel since the 21st of October, 1941. The aircraft, Spitfire W3327, was shot down 4 miles off Boulogne whilst on a rescue mission.

BULL BAITING

The 'sport' of Bull Baiting is said to have been one of the oldest public events carried out in Horsham. It took place usually on the 21st of December (St. Thomas's Day) within the boundaries of the Carfax and involved securing the bull to a metal ring in the road. From here on the animal was teased by the crowd that was made up mainly of the rougher elements of the population.
 If by any chance the poor animal was killed whilst being annoyed in this way then the meat was sold at a low rate 'by the candle' on the 'Butchers Row', (Middle Street). Some stories tell that on occasion the bull would break loose from his rope and chase those engaged in attacking it around the town centre forcing some to take refuge in trees.
 At one time in 1814 a group of well meaning individuals tried to put a stop to the practice but they felt the wrath of those who enjoyed the pastime. Those in favour of baiting claimed that the animals even enjoyed it and sighted as evidence an occasion where a bull wandered up from Chesworth fields 'looking for entertainment'.
 In the end the custom became less popular, it finally being outlawed by act of Parliament in the year 1835. But die-hards still insisted that bull meat tasted better if the animal to be eaten had been teased a little before slaughter!

 Bull Bating is also said to have been enjoyed in Henfield at the time. The remains of an iron ring and post used to secure the animal were unearthed by builders in a field opposite the George Inn. Cock-fighting was also enjoyed hereabouts as well as in Southwater.

MICK MILES RACE

Over the years many stories have come from the forest of St Leonard's. Perhaps the most well known concerns the notorious smuggler Mick Miles. Mick is said to have challenged the Devil to a race along a mile long track after his 'Satanic Majesty' had tried to carry off the man (presumably for his wicked deeds). Seeing Old Nick's age Mick felt sure he would win the race and his freedom and so this proved as legend has it the Devil was left fully a quarter of a mile behind.
 Watched by many spirits allied to the Devil Mick won the race hands down and declared that Satan was no match for the likes of him and should be gone from the forest. Surprisingly old Nick kept to his side of the bargain and departed with his gruesome band of spirits in tow. Needless to say the track along which the race was held is to this day known as Mick Miles Race.
 It is worth mentioning that some older texts give the smugglers surname as 'Mills', and not Miles.

THE DRAGON OF ST. LEONARD'S FOREST

In the year 1614, John Trundle of London printed details that stated that a 'strange and monstrous serpent or dragon lately discovered in St Leonard's forest slaughters both men and cattle'.
'In Sussex there is a pretty market towne called Horsham, near which is a forrest called St Leonard's Forrest, and there in a vast and unfrequented place, heathie, vaultie, full of unwholesome shades and overgrown hollowes where this serpent is thought to be bred, certaine and too true it is that there it yet lives, within 3 or 4 miles compass are its usual haunts, oftentimes at a place called Fay-gate, and it hath been seene within halfe a mile of Horsham, a wonder, no doubt, most terrible and noisome to the inhabitants thereabouts'.
He goes on to say that the creature leaves behind it a 'glutinous trail and slimie matter' such as that left by a snail. This matter is described as being all right to touch but very foul to the nose.
Further details describe the dragon as being over nine feet in length and shaped narrowly at both ends with a 'quantitie of thickness in the middest'. The neck of the serpent was 'about an ell long with a white ring about it' and scales (black and red in colour) covered its back and belly.
The nature of the dragon was said to be arrogant. On hearing people approach he is said to have raised up his head and challenged them by sometimes spitting poisonous venom in their direction. 'This he can throw up to '4 roddes distance from himself and on occasion he has killed a man and a woman who are said to have swelled up to a great size in death'.
John Steele, Christopher Holder and an old widow from Fay-gate bear witness to this.

Local historians write that the story of the Dragon came from 'poetic legend' which asserts St Leonard himself fought with a 'mighty worm in the foreste,' and wherever his blood fell during the battle there sprung up lilies of the valley.
With several other people of the period writing of Dragons being brought to Paris and others being slain at Sancton one wonders if there wasn't some foundation to the myth after all. To this day prehistoric creatures that were thought to be long extinct occasionally turn up in some unusual location and baffle the living daylights out of scientists.
Perhaps it wouldn't be all that foolish to suggest that some larger animals survived in our dense forests up until a few hundred years ago. When David Attenborough went in search of dragons back in the 1960s he found a large lizard creature resident on a remote island off Indonesian. This animal was very dragon-like from its curved and grinning mouth down to its yellow and pink forked tongue which could have been mistaken as fire by someone who didn't know better.
Prehistoric remains dug up from Tilgate forest in 1825 by Gidean Mantell were found to be those of a giant iguanodon. Later, between January, 1939 and February, 1941, more remains of this same creature were unearthed at Clock House Brick Works, situated about six miles away from Horsham. Remains were also found at Faygate.
Though much of the forest has disappeared over the years, due mainly to the two world wars, large tracts still remain for those hardy souls brave enough to venture forth in search of adventure and perhaps even dragons....

ROOST HOLE REPTILE

Most towns can lay claim to a big fish or two and Horsham is no exception. Ask any fishermen down at Roost Hole pond whether it's O.K. to dangle your toes in the water and they'll reply with a firm: 'No!'
If you choose to ignore their advice you may very well get to meet the fish that some locals have nicknamed, 'the Alligator.' Weighing in at around 35lbs last time it was caught, this monster Pike has been known to swallow cruising ducks whole.
Anyone who deliberately goes after this brute should beware. Hooking into it is said to be like ensnaring a speedboat.

MILL POND MONSTERS

Warnham Mill pond is another local water said to contain some very big Pike. One Horsham angler related a story that supposedly happened many years ago concerning one of these fish. An old lady was strolling along the edge of the pool with her Jack Russell Terrier when the animal decided to paddle a short distance into the water. No sooner had it done so when a large Pike shot from the water, grabbed the dog in its sharp teeth and dragged him under. The Terrier was never seen again.
It is said that if you look down over Warnham Mill Bridge you can sometimes see these monster fish as they venture out from their nature reserve and swim up Red River.

WILD DOGS AND DRUNKS ... IN CHURCH!

In days gone by Horsham was plagued by wild dogs to such an extent that the Vicar of St. Mary's church was forced to employ a dog warden to keep the sometimes aggressive creatures from his aisles. Churchwardens accounts for 1643, show that James Long was paid 10d for scaring the animals away.
Records for 1646 show that the Horsham churchwardens didn't only have trouble with dogs. It was all too common for people to attend services in a state that was considered improper for the purposes of worshipping. Fines for drunkenness were in the region of 5s. Swearing cost you 12d.

HORSHAM FAIRS

These town fairs, of which there were several each year, were very popular with the people of Horsham. One main event was held each July in the Carfax and involved much merrymaking. The entire town centre was filled with booths of every sort imaginable including plenty that served strong drink. Some house owners even got in on the act by turning their dwellings into temporary drinking establishments by placing a bushel of wheat over their doors. These places were known as 'Bough' houses.
Fights were always a regular occurrence at these fairs, much to the annoyance of some living nearby, but in 1835 things got out of control when a mass of fights developed into a gigantic brawl. Unable to control events by any other way a local official was forced to read the Riot Act from the steps of the Town Hall.

RIDICULE ON ST. CRISPIN'S DAY

St.Crispin was the Patron of shoemakers and in Horsham those engaged in this profession celebrated the 25th of October with much merrymaking. Other townsfolk enjoyed the day because of a tradition that said you could ridicule or humiliate anyone who had publicly misbehaved over the last year.
Effigies of these people were made, taken to the areas where they lived and hung on the signs outside local public houses. Come the 5th of November they were taken down and burnt on bonfires.

THE BEGGAR-POOKER

The Beggar-Pooker was a man employed by the people of Horsham to see off beggars. When troubled by one of these rascals a gentleman would call to the official to 'Pook him off'. This would be done with a sturdy stick that was continually shoved in the direction of the beggar thus forcing him away.
One story concerning this activity is described in the Recollections of Henry Burstow. He tells that his brother had cause to visit Guildford one day and whilst there was accosted by a beggar.
This man asked if the Horsham Beggar-Pooker was still operating in the town. Burstow's brother replied that the Pooker, named Potter, had died some time earlier to which the beggar said,' then I can go back to Horsham again.'

He then went on to tell how Potter had seen him off some years before by Pooking him all the way down the Bishopric. Once outside the town he had turned and swung a fist at the official knocking him head over heels and then ran away as fast as he could to Guildford.

WIVES, BOUGHT AND SOLD!

In 1820, a man called Smart sold his wife at Horsham market to a man called Steere from Billingshurst. He paid 3/6 for her but found after a time that she had 'qualities' he did not like. He re-sold her to a man named Greenfield who lived with her until his death.

Trouble occurred for a journeyman-blacksmith who sold his wife and two children for £2.5.0. Several bystanders reported him to a local magistrate causing all concerned to leave town quickly. The last time this happened was in 1844 when Ann Holland was purchased by a man from Southwater for £1.10.0. A celebration followed but in the end the buyer, a Mr. Johnson, was disappointed when his new wife ran away and married someone else.

HORSHAM ELECTIONS, THE TALK OF THE COUNTRY

During the General Election of 1847, Horsham became the most talked about town in the country. Bribery and corruption took place on such a scale as to be unbelievable. The two men fighting for votes, Seymour Fitzgerald (pink party) and John Jervis (blue party), set up their headquarters in the Anchor and the Kings Head and set about gaining power any way they could. With much drink being ready to hand they each started to give away as much as possible causing the Brighton Gazette to write that,' Horsham was deluged with drink.'

Its rival, the Herald, wrote that,' the electors have been disgraced in the face of the country.'

At the time Horsham's only constable reported, 'I never in my life before saw such a drunken and riotous scene.'

While most of the town were blind drunk, Henry Padwick, an agent for the former M.P., Mr Hurst, offered Fitzgerald the seat for £1000 as long as he brought the former minister's house. Soon after this almost all the publicans were instructed to give free drink to whoever promised their vote. Fitzgerald held a meeting in the Swan and handed out 124 bottles of wine and three dozen (36!) bowls of punch. It was said that local people never brought a drink themselves for the whole six weeks of the election campaign.

As well as offering drink the prospective M.P.s brought votes with hard cash. In the House of Commons it was stated that an agent of Jervis, a Mr James, had sat in the Crown Public House with a bag of gold to impress the voters. Meanwhile, Jervis's father (who just happened to be the Attorney-General) visited local landowners and offered them various high offices if they would force their tenants to vote for his son.

Another one of the so called dirty tricks involved getting your opponent's voters so drunk that they incapable of even standing, let alone voting. In the end Jervis won the election but the result was overturned by a committee and another contest ordered.

At the time the then Prime Minister, Lord John Russell, introduced a bill ' To promote further enquiry into Bribery and Corruption alleged to prevail in the Borough of Horsham'. This idea was eventually dropped as the honourable members felt such an inquest may uncover more than it was meant to. Nothing changes does it?

NOTE: In the years 1333, 1345 and 1421, Horsham M.P.s were indicted for burglary, deer-stealing and assault. Most escaped without punishment.

A HANGING AT THE ANCHOR INN, HORSHAM

In July, 1749, the Horsham Executioner, Robert Clarke, hanged himself in the hayloft of the Anchor Inn. He elected to use a bridle instead of the usual rope. It is said he committed suicide after gambling away half a guinea he had been entrusted with to buy a pig.

The Anchor was also the scene of some nasty incidents involving animals. One incident involved a group of men who, after laying money down against a cat's survival, tied a rock around its neck and threw it into a mill stream. Those who wagered the cat would escape its predicament won the bet.
John Baker, of Horsham Park House, recorded that in February, 1773, the pub's bull mastiff killed six lambs and was promptly put to death by its owner.

THE BANK ROBBERY OF 1840

On the 13th of February, 1840, a bank in West Street was robbed of £450 hard cash. The crafty thieves broke into the house of the manager, sneaked up stairs, and stole the keys right out from under his pillow as he slept. Once in the bank the criminals bagged the money and sat down to a feast of wine and ham. Before dawn broke they had disappeared leaving behind them only a few scraps of meat and several empty bottles.
The gang were never caught.

MURDER IN THE TOWN

In times gone by drinking and gambling were said to have been prevalent in Horsham. Being as it was a market town many people from outlying districts used to regularly converge to do business.
For rest and recreation they retired to their favourite public houses which are listed as being The 'King's Head, 'Anchor', 'Black Horse', 'Swan', 'Punch Bowl', 'Green Dragon' and 'Hurst Arms' which was also known as 'The Black Jug'.
At one less frequented pub, 'The Queen's Head', there occurred on the night of Saturday the 8th, March 1830, a murder. It seems a group of men fell out over a game of cards and started fighting amongst themselves. The Landlord broke up the group and ejected the party from his establishment only to see two of the combatants, Henry Hewett and Edward Smith continue their argument.
The two men then engaged in another fight that lasted for several minutes until Hewett produced a knife and stabbed Smith. Fifteen minutes later the victim was dead and Hewett found himself resident in the town gaol. He was tried on the 30th of March and found guilty of manslaughter only. Escaping the gallows he was transported to Bermuda for life but managed to return after only ten years away.

PRECAUTIONS TAKEN AGAINST GRAVE ROBBERS

In the early nineteenth century England had become plagued by the evil craft of grave robbing. Doctors were demanding ever greater numbers of deceased so that they could experiment with the bodies. As the only bodies that were of any real use to them had to be fresh it became the custom, for those that could afford it, to hire night-watchmen to keep guard over the graves of the recently departed.
In Horsham men were employed in this profession to guard against the 'Resurrection Men' or body-snatchers. They would spend long nights in the graveyard receiving payments of around 2s. 6d or 5s.

THE PLAGUE HITS TOWN

In the years 1560, 1574, 1608 and 1609 the Black Death laid its deadly hand on the town of Horsham. It is believed that 111 people died in 1560 but this number declined on subsequent outbreaks.

The plague was carried by fleas who were in turn carried by the rats. After the victim was bitten and infected with the Black Death there would be an incubation period lasting from two to ten days. When this period of time is up the sufferer would have begun to get a fever. From this stage onward the Plague could be spread by the slightest cough or sneeze which would put infected droplets of water into the air.

Those unfortunate enough to 'catch their death' died horribly.

The Town was also visited by Small Pox in 1803 and 1832.

WITCHES IN HORSHAM

In 1575 Margaret Cooper of Kirdford was found guilty of bewitching three people who all died. She was brought to Horsham and hanged to death.

Come 1577, Alice Casseloew of Mayfield was found guilty of causing an ox to die by putting curses on it. She was sentenced to a year in gaol but died before she was released.

In the Year 1680, the last woman was tried for witchcraft in Horsham. Her name was Alice Nash and on the 22nd of July she was accused of having bewitched a child, Elizabeth Slater, who was only two and a half years old. The child died on the 21st of February that year. There was also another charge relating to the dead girl's sister.

Fortunately for Alice Nash she was found not guilty by a petty jury and released soon after.

One such story of which there were many came from a small village near Horsham and concerned the deeds of a woman reputed to be a witch. During a funeral procession the woman in question was heard to say that she was going to take a short cut to the church. At this point it seems she vanished from sight only to reappear when the coffin reached its final resting place, the church graveyard.

During her absence all those mourners carrying the coffin swore that it became considerably heavier for the exact duration that the old woman was missing. Locals say that she dematerialised herself and hitched a free ride to the church in the coffin.

All the laws against witchcraft were repealed in 1747.

THE SOLDIERS OF HORSHAM TOWN

The Duke of Wellington is reported to have said of his troops that, ' they are the scum of the earth,' and, ' they should frighten Napoleon because, by God, they frighten me! '

If the good people of Horsham did not know what he meant before his soldiers were stationed in the town, they most certainly did after. The men who arrived looked nothing like the chocolate box soldiers we imagine today. It was written of the troopers who stayed in Horsham that: ' They produced a state of immorality bad enough to be incredible. The state of mentality was worse than is conceived of. It produced dishonesty in every shape among moneyed individuals etc...'

Before a proper barracks was built for the soldiers in Horsham they were forced to camp out on the area known as the Common.

In 1782 the 52nd Foot were stationed in Horsham and it was not long before they, like the few before them, began to make their presence felt.

Whilst some joined local footpads (muggers) and set about robbing unfortunate travellers and farmers returning from market, others tried their luck at a little burglary. Moving quietly into town at night they succeeded in breaking into the Green Dragon Public House and robbing it of £10. But the culprits were identified as soldiers after bayonet marks were found around the point of entry. A Colonel offered a five pound reward for information and was rewarded when a private admitted the crime. His accomplices were drummed out of the regiment and sent to a man-of-war but the soldier was given 150 lashes and the five pounds reward!

When the town barracks was eventually built it was decided to situate it in the Tower Hill area. Residents living nearby the site later began complaining as the screams of some soldiers being punished at the whipping post was quite disturbing. This was not surprising as some of the servicemen were getting up to 600 strokes for their crimes. These grumbles at the army had no effect as whipping went on until 1836.

In 1795, three soldiers from the Oxford Militia were hanged for stealing flour and wheat. Many others involved escaped with lesser punishments. Two years later Horsham soldiers attended a Pedlars Fair in Slinfold and caused a disturbance whilst drunk. The men tore down several stalls, shouted abuse and took over a pub in which they broke all the china tankards and plates. On their way back to town they broke into a pub in Broadbridge Heath and stole some bacon.

From the moment the barracks went up the disturbances caused by the soldiers started to rise. Records show that in 1797 there were two uprisings by troops stationed at Horsham. The first was started when two soldiers from the Derbyshire Regiment were locked in the guardroom for complaining about their food. Their friends and members of the Bedfordshire Regiment attempted a rescue at ten o'clock that night but turned back when they realised they would be forced to fight against others armed with cannons loaded with grape shot.

The second incident involved drunken members of the Surrey Militia who attempted to free a friend from the same guardroom. Cavalry had to be brought in to quell this disturbance.

In July 1798, a group of twelve soldiers stopped the Horsham and Worthing Carrier, a man named Sadler, and robbed him of the goods on his wagon. Once they had what they wanted they let him go on his way.

The Crabtree Inn in Lower Beeding was visited by strolling soldiers in 1799. They asked for some food but the Landlady was unable or unwilling to provide it so the men decided to leave. At this moment their attention was attracted by a beautiful caged canary bird that had begun to sing. One of the soldiers quickly produced some money and asked if the bird was for sale. The woman dithered for a moment but finally named a price of half a guinea. Before she could change her mind the soldier slapped down the money on the counter, opened the cage, took out the bird and wrung its neck. As the poor Landlady stood with her mouth gaping the trooper handed the bird back to her and demanded that it be plucked and cooked for them to eat. A short time later the servicemen sat down to a 'delicate feast'.

In the same year a drunken corporal of the Hereford Regiment fell from an upstairs window at the barracks and broke his neck.

Severe crimes committed in 1800 caused three Irish soldiers, John Cullen, Patrick Shea and Michael Donellin to be hanged on Horsham Common before a crowd of 1000 people. Before dying one of the soldiers shouted that, 'the Hangman was trembling more than he was.'

These men were possibly members of an Irish Rifle Regiment that reportedly ran riot at the barracks around this time stabbing fellow troopers of the 13th Foot with bayonets. Several of their victims almost died.

With the town banks unwilling to take soldiers' money and with no entertainment available in their quarters they were forced to spend their spare time in Horsham's many public houses.

With soldiers being paid as much as £7.10s 0d each this meant much hard drinking and many fights. When a fight did start that involved soldiers it was usually a hard affair to stop. The Town Constables frequently found that they were simply outnumbered on these occasions and so had to call on the help of the townsfolk. During these mass fights the commonly heard cry of 'Hurrah for Hell or Horsham', was often used. Many brawls were started by poor farm labourers who, after working long days in the fields for a pittance, became jealous of the amount of money the soldiers had to spend.

It was common practice for women to follow soldiers around the country in the nineteenth century. And so when a new regiment marched into Horsham town they inevitably brought with them their wives and girlfriends. Records show that on the 20th of January, 1806, a regimental surgeon helped two women give birth as they entered the town with a body of soldiers. One woman had her baby in the back of a baggage wagon whilst the other had her child delivered at an inn.

In the month of August, 1807, five hundred men from a Lancashire Militia ran riot in Horsham after a long march up from the coast. After fighting their way along most of the route these soldiers rested up, along with their women, at the Stopham Bridge Inn. But when the Landlord ran out of food and drink they destroyed the establishment, breaking every item they could lay their hands on. On arriving in Horsham they were paid by their superiors and immediately retired to the local ale houses. After three days of drinking (one pub took over £200) the soldiers seemed to go mad and attacked property and livestock in the Carfax. Wagons and carriages travelling through the town were attacked and overturned and orchards stripped before some sort of order returned. It is thought this massive drinking binge took place either in The Crown or The Lamb and Shepherdess which stood where King and Chasemore now stands.

Officers of the regiment paid compensation of £10 each to the victims of this riot. This money was split between the poor and those that needed it to make repairs. One soldier involved in the riots is even said to have approached the Governor of the Gaol and asked to be hanged. The Governor refused and the private persuaded some friends to string him up from a Carfax tree. He was rescued just in time as his face turned black in colour.

Fig. 5. Soldiers march on Horsham to do battle with the townsfolk, 1814.

A letter dated April 30th, 1814, also mentions another riot that took place within the town. 'There has been sad work between the soldiers and the townspeople. About 250 of the former attacked the town with clubs, stones, etc., but were repulsed.' One assumes that the soldiers must have had a real grievance against the people of the town to organise such an attack as this. Perhaps they were banned from a number of establishments for a period they felt to be unjust.

But it was not just privates who caused trouble in the town. When two officers fell out in their mess hall they decided to fight a duel on the Common. But both men survived the encounter with no wounds due to the fact that they were both incredibly bad shots.

Another incident that involved the use of firearms happened when a young officer of the 64th Foot named Bunn, attempted to murder George Stanton in a Horsham street. Ensign Bunn had been having an affair with Stanton's wife and it seems he was over taken with emotion on coming face to face with her husband. Fortunately for Stanton he escaped death when the pistol misfired. The two men then commenced to fight each other before a growing crowd until the affray was broken up and the two combatants summoned to appear in court in Chichester. Bunn had the cheek to blame Stanton for the altercation but missed the hearing because his unit was posted abroad. He was later captured and sentenced to spend one month in prison for assault.

Although the soldiers caused the people of Horsham much bother they did on occasions amuse them as well. With more money than sense some men actually lit their pipes with £1 notes whilst others mixed them with brandy and gingerbread and ate them from potties. One man is even reported to have cooked a pocket watch in a frying pan.

Whilst the East Kent regiment was stationed in the area several of its members wagered that a colleague couldn't eat two dozen five ounce gooseberry tarts in half an hour. He attempted the task but after twenty three minutes and seventeen tarts he was forced to retire with a sickness and violent nose bleed.

Church records show that during the period that the army were stationed at barrack fields around 450 men died.

THE STOCKS

The stocks used to stand on Gaol Green, an area very close to where the current bandstand is.
The last person to occupy them was one Charley Price who was known locally as 'Patch Price'. Described as an ugly little brass-whisker'd man with a club foot, he is said to have worn a pot hat, white smock, drab breeches and white socks. It was his habit to spend all his money on drink and then parade up and down the road outside his sister's home swearing loudly and shouting for money.
It appears he was regularly put in the stocks to sober up, the last time being in the year 1834. These original stocks were destroyed one November the 5th bonfire night (by Price?) and a new set had to be commissioned. These however were never used and were kept towards the south end of the town hall.
During redevelopment of the Carfax recently a new pair of stocks have been erected for sightseers a little away from the original site.

ROAD INSPECTORS AND FOOTPADS

These were in effect robbers who attacked travellers on the dark and lonely roads around Horsham. There are many accounts of such crimes and we list but a few below:-

Saturday, 21st, December, 1801, Mr. Anthony Widden was stopped by four men and robbed of £40 in notes and gold.
Thursday, 20th, January, 1802, Mr. Cremer, master waggoner, was grabbed by two men, taken into his house and robbed of £40 in cash and several pieces of silver. Before the men left they stole two guineas from the maid. They were never seen again.
2nd, January, 1803, Mr. Thomas Ansell was on his way back from Horsham market when he was stopped by the Dog and Bacon and threatened. Being a big man Ansell fought off the individual who ran away over the Common. On the same night a Mr. Knight, a farmer from Bourne Hill was knocked down and robbed of three £1 notes and a 7s. gold piece. Later that year yet another farmer was robbed of £58 but this obviously illiterate road inspector was caught after he tried to pass one of the five pound notes thinking it was only a one pound note. This naturally aroused suspicions and he was marched off to gaol.
10th, February, 1807, saw a Mr. Ireland robbed of £72 in notes. His assailants escaped unpunished.

Fig. 6. Two 'Road Inspectors' prepare to rob a farmer on the outskirts of Horsham.

A BRIEF HISTORY OF HORSHAM GAOL

Horsham Gaol, mentioned in a survey in 1611, and known to have been in existence way back in 1532, was originally situated in the area of North Street. Later it was moved to the north-east corner of the Carfax but in 1640 it was moved again to where the main Post Office now stands. Many people complained about the Gaol house being in the Carfax and in 1779 it was decided to move it for a fourth time. This time it was built in Queen Street, just past the north end of where the iron bridge stands today.

After the Napoleonic wars crime soared as soldiers and sailors returned to a country which could not properly support them. Unable to find work on the land which had been largely neglected and mismanaged they all to easily fell into a life of crime. To cope with the increase in prisoners Horsham Gaol was enlarged in 1819 but these improvements were not enough to stop Lewes taking the assizes away in 1830. From that time on only debtors and the condemned stayed at the prison in any numbers.

The prison was sold in 1845 to Henry Michell for the sum of £2,560. To this day some shop keepers in the area still have items such as cell doors stored away on their property.

THE DEBTORS

The debtors that were imprisoned in the town gaol had a rough time of it before conditions became better in 1779. They petitioned Parliament in 1718, 1724 and 1736 complaining of distress and starvation. The prison reformer, John Howard, remarked at the time that the gaol was stinking and corrupt and that the inmates saw no light and had no straw to sleep on. Collections were sometimes made in the town just to buy food for the debtors.

THE LONGEST PRISONER

In 1810, Simon Southward died in Horsham Prison after spending 43 years locked up there for debt. During his stay there he insisted on being called the Earl of Derby. Fellow inmates always addressed him as, 'My Lord.'

THE FIRST QUAKER TO BE IMPRISONED

On the 24th of June, 1665, Thomas Laycock was put into a dark, damp cell at Horsham Gaol for four months after, 'going into the steeplehouse of Horsham on a first day of the week and speaking some words of Christian exhortation after the priest had done.' Laycock had been found guilty of shouting 'Thou lyar!' at the priest and calling him, 'a ravening Wolfe in sheep's clothing,' and saying that, 'he was the Anti-Christ.'

BEAR BAITING

The practice of bear baiting took place throughout England until all baiting was subject to prohibition in 1835. In reality the 'sport' died out some years earlier as the availability of European bears dried up. Puritans also helped outlawing this cruellest of activities stating that, like all other baiting, it was unkind in the extreme. But evidence suggests other factors motivated them in this matter. Baiting was popular on Sundays and encouraged drinking and gambling. As with bull baiting, meetings took place in Market Square, near to the Bear Public House. The bear itself would have one of its hind legs tethered to a large stake with a strong chain. Interested participants would then unleash their huge English bulldogs, which would attack the unfortunate creature while all about, fuelled by alcohol, cheered the animals on. If spectators were lucky, extra entertainment was provided by wickedly imaginative individuals who would think nothing of throwing pepper up the nostrils of the already infuriated bears (and bulls) causing them to go mad. Others even added more exotic animals to draw in the crowds. It was not unknown for monkeys to be tied to the backs of dogs and bulls. Although the baiting of animals was banned earlier in the century this didn't stop the good people of Horsham displaying a dancing bear in the Market Square as late as 1893. The outlawing of baiting sports only encouraged the breeding of dogs specifically for fighting. A result of this was the introduction of the Staffordshire Bull terrier, an animal with the viciousness and quickness of the terrier and the strength of the bulldog.

THOSE WHO 'BROKE THE GAOL'

It was 8pm on the 22nd of February, 1739, when eleven men broke out of Horsham gaol and escaped into the night. Their plan had been a simple and effective one that involved ordering a large amount of beer from the pub next door. The guard, called a Turnkey, got the drink for the group and then found that he was unable to get the sizeable container through the bars of the cell. As planned, he opened the door and was immediately flattened as the men ran over him to freedom. Only one, Andrew Gatland was caught. 1765 saw another successful escape when four men, recently reprieved from the gallows and awaiting transportation to the colonies, decided they would rather stay in England. Only one of their number was caught and he was banished from the country for fourteen years. In 1773, John Stacey and John Dabbs, both burglars, and John Parker, sawed through their irons and dug a hole to escape. Two other prisoners were unhappy to find that their shoulders were too big to allow them to follow. Stacey and Dabbs were later recaptured but Parker was never seen again. A prison inspection by John Howard in 1774 uncovered a large pile of rubble uncovered by some tunnelling villains. Luckily for Howard the prisoners did not attack him as he made his discovery. Another attempt was foiled in 1777 when two prisoners who were not brought in on a plan told the guards of it. Mary West, an insane inmate, escaped from a top floor window by jumping into the courtyard and running away. She was found hiding in a ditch on Horsham Common and retaken. Friday, 18th December, 1802, saw William Comer and Whalley Beatson attack their Turnkey and lock him in their cell. Out in the courtyard they threw a rope made from strips of their blankets over the wall. On finding them not in their cells the Gaoler raised the town and sent them off in all directions to catch the mail robber and horse thief. Early next morning the Gaoler was told of some strange noises heard in the night by a group of debtors also resident in the prison. Another search revealed the 'escapees' to be hiding in the cesspit, their bodies more than half covered by the horrible contents. They had planned to escape after the surrounding area had been fully searched. The last escape was made by Richard Sheppard, a man with nothing to lose as he had been sentenced to death. When a door was left open in the exercise yard he quickly ran through it and disappeared. Search parties turned up nothing but a passer by named Killick, saw Sheppard as he climbed from a drain hole directly in front of the prison. The escapee was quickly apprehended by Killick who later claimed a £20 reward for his efforts. At the time of his capture Sheppard had offered him a bribe to let him go saying, 'for God's sake, let me go or I shall be hung.'

WHIPPING

During the sixteenth, seventeenth and eighteenth centuries numerous criminals were whipped or lashed with the 'cat'. These poor unfortunates were either tied to a whipping post or the back of a wagon before receiving their punishment.

In December of 1686, John Ward succeeded in gaining some money from Gregory Haines and Richard Whittington under false pretences. Tried in Arundel, Ward was found guilty and sentenced to be pilloried in that town and whipped at the carts tail in Storrington and Horsham. The route taken by his cart here stretched between the church and the gaol.

1772 saw Thomas Wilson convicted of stealing 24 pairs of shoe buckles. For this he was condemned to be whipped until his body was bloody.

Another man destined to feel the lash across his back was Richard Denyer. Convicted at Horsham in July, 1785, of stealing sixteen feet of oak plank in Heyshott, Denyer spent three months in gaol before being fastened to a wagon and whipped around the market place.

Records show that on the 10th of February, 1751, the, 'Master of the House of Correction,' William Ede, received 5d for whipping ten vagrants.

THE LAST WHIPPING

In 1805, it was reported that the last public flogging had taken place in Horsham. A man by the name of Feist was convicted of stealing wine and thereafter tied to a wagon and hauled through the town. Unfortunately the Gaoler could find no one strong and willing to carry out the lashing and the job was eventually given to an old man who was so decrepit that his efforts at whipping left no marks whatsoever.

After this episode the whole idea of punishing criminals in this way was abandoned in Horsham.

SMUGGLING IN AND AROUND HORSHAM

No other counties in all of England saw quite as much smuggling as Kent and Sussex did in the days of old. Everyone from the poorest to the richest seems to have profited in one way or another from this most hazardous of trades.

One such person was a respected solicitor who used his coachman, Bob Reading, to distribute the casks of spirits, called 'pigs' around the Horsham area. These 'pigs' were dropped off after dark in the stables situated where Albion Way is today. The solicitors supplier was a certain Jack Akehurst of Copthorne who would bring down and unload his illicit cargo of 25 two gallon casks after dark and be well on his way home before dawn broke.

The local Ostler, name of Waterman, was often seen carrying buckets of hogwash about town. If any Exciseman had cared to inspect his containers closely they would have found that they contained a 'pig' of spirits each hidden beneath false bottoms. Several local magistrates and the vicar were said to be amongst his customers.

Another local man named Parker, who lived in a cottage on the Common, was a very popular fellow at the time due to the fact that he used his house as an unofficial distillery. Situated on or near where Athelstan Way is today Parker played host to many people from the surrounding area who liked to pop over for a tipple of the hard stuff.

One of Parker's close relatives was a well known local Owler (smuggler) known by his nickname as 'Old Saucey Elliot'. This man, his face badly scarred, apparently distributed alcohol around Horsham for his nephew, stopping at the Bishopric, Robin Hood Lane and finally Friday Street where a trusted customer had a hiding place secreted away in the woods nearby.

With two sons Elliot ran a gang that worked the Cowfold and Nuthurst areas. One of their main assets was a horse that was trained to find its way home if it were ever to get separated from its owners. This could be especially handy if they were surprised by Excisemen with the animal fully loaded.

Another local man who liked a bit of smuggling was called Aylward. This man was known to have trained his horse to lie down on its side incase he were ever in danger of being spotted whilst out and about. His secret hiding place for drink was in an old tomb that stood in the graveyard near to the Barracks. He and his wife made a tidy sum selling spirits to the soldiers, she smuggling the drink to them under the folds of her petticoats.

Charles Hoare was another who felt nothing at using church property as a safe place to keep his 'refreshment'. Living in one of the Hayler cottages situated along the Worthing Road he would stash the contraband in the baptistry of the chapel itself always being careful to remove it come Whitsun.

If you were part of a smuggling operation the one thing you could not do without would be a good hiding place. A cottage in old Tan Yard Lane had a small basement cleverly built under its fireplace that was big enough to store a large amount of banned merchandise and a hidden panel was said also to exist between The Prince of Wales in West Street and a house next door. Other properties at the end of West Street are said to have cellars that were linked for the purpose of smuggling. The Original Norfolk Arms, that stands on the Forest road, is said to have natural sandstone caves underneath it that may or may not have been used to hide untaxed items away from the Revenue men.

One of the largest concealed tunnels ever discovered in Horsham leads from the site of old the Malthouse that was situated in Springfield Road. Uncovered during the demolition of the storage house, once owned by the Allen Brothers, it was found to lead under the roadway to a nearby field. Wagons, their wheels made quiet with sacking, were secretly filled here with 'duty free' malt, and noiselessly pulled away to London in the dead of night. The Allen brothers were eventually found out and fined £110,000 but they managed to escape to America. As England had no extradition treaty with the United States the solicitor general was forced to reduce the amount to £10,000. The brothers paid up and returned home.

A different kind of underground hideout to that of the tunnel was the Bell Hole. These excavations were originally dug so that iron ore could be brought up but they were later used by smugglers for hiding their 'goods'. Looking on the surface very much like a well, these holes in fact opened up as their name suggests to the shape of a bell. If two or more of these vertical mines were dug close to one another passages would be bored through the earth to join them together. The woods around Colgate and Forest road are said to be home to some of these strange holes. Some were also discovered in Surrey and Croydon but these were called Dene or Dane holes by the people thereabouts.

Another smuggler, this time from Upper Beeding, was reported to hide his ill gotten gains in a hollow tree next to the graveyard. Years later, on the day of the man's funeral, his coffin was about to be taken through the cemetery gates when a violent wind brought his hollow tree crashing down on the entrance. Needless to say this in turn brought many knowing looks from members of his family.

With many of these hiding places built over the years it is very possible that several have gone undiscovered to this very day. You yourself may even be sitting in a house at this very moment that has other 'accommodating' spaces secreted about it!

But the gangs that carried out the smuggling needed more than just hiding places. Travelling up from the coast with large amounts of booty was thirsty work and if anyone was kind enough to offer a little hospitality it would be seized upon at once. One such resting place was said to be Springfield Farm. On some nights thirty or forty armed men would ride into the courtyard, dismount and head straight for the servants quarters where they would be offered refreshment. Outside their horses would be watered and fed or even exchanged for less tired animals.

Anyone looking at a map of Horsham today will see that one of the ponds within St. Leonard's Forest is named Hawkins Pond. This name comes from the leader of a gang of smugglers who operated in the area.

Another who dabbled in smuggling was John Fuller of Mannings Heath. A charcoal burner and part time maker of brooms, Fuller aroused no suspicion when he travelled around the lanes and country tracks surrounding Horsham touting his goods. Little did Customs men know that beneath the coal and cleaning utensils piled high on his cart lay hidden many kegs of spirit. It was known that Fuller also stored hundreds of gallons of brandy under the floorboards of his home at the Goldings. The family are said to have become rich to the tune of several thousand pounds due to their smuggling activities.

Fig. 7. A Horsham smuggler going about his business by night.

The village of West Grinstead was home to two men who could rightly call themselves experts at smuggling. Downer and Nailard specialised in running booty up from the coast and became rich men during the process. But it is said that both men made the fatal mistake of over indulging in the goods they moved. They both died from excess drinking.

One fact worth mentioning about Downer was that he had a blind horse. This animal would, if doped with raw beef soaked in brandy, run anything up to sixty miles a day at amazing speeds.

Presumably this was very handy if you were likely to have the government men chasing you.

In 1747 the notorious Hawkhurst gang committed a crime that would eventually see several of its members hanged for murder. After storming the Customs house in Poole to recapture £500 of tea that had been taken from them the gang had a member recognised by a local man named Chater. The gang got to hear that he was about to give evidence against them and captured him along with a customs man by the name of Galley.

After having their faces slashed both men were taken out into the night and done away with in an extremely brutal fashion. Galley was buried alive in a sandpit and Chater, after being kept chained to a barn wall for three days was finally dropped head first down a well. The smugglers finished him off by dropping large rocks down after him.

The smugglers responsible were captured and held under heavy guard in Horsham gaol.

Eye witness reports say that during their stay in the town these men were allowed to attend church services. Their faces a picture of dejection they were made to stand in the middle aisle, a place where other church goers couldn't fail to miss them as they stood in their leg irons and chains.

They left town in January of 1749 and were taken under guard to Chichester. Apart from one smuggler named Jackson who died prematurely, they were all hanged and four of their number gibbeted.

Records show that in 1772 there was a battle on Wimbledon Common between Customs men and a group of around thirty smugglers all of whom came from Horsham. The bandits retreated to Horsham but were followed all the way back, one of their number being killed in the town itself. On this occasion the government men won the fight and took possession of 800 pounds of tea.

One year later two customs officers were enticed out from Horsham only to be taken prisoners by a gang numbering around sixty men. The agents were then beaten up and told they were about to die by their own guns. Fortunately for the two men it was a wet day and the power in their pistols refused to go off. Frustrated by this unexpected snag the smugglers settled on beating up the men for a second time and left them for dead. They were found some hours later in a very sorry condition.

In 1777 goods captured from smugglers in the Horsham district were transported to the Customs house in Shoreham and auctioned off. During this year alone 24,000 gallons of spirits and 80,000 tons of tea were sold in this way. Thirty three years earlier at Pevensey, 500 packhorses were used to carry illicit goods unloaded from three cutters. Records declare that around one quarter of the country's overseas trade was being smuggled at this time.

It is recorded that on the 6th of December, 1778, a group of around 200 smugglers rode through Henfield. They had with them seven captured Customs men.

At around 1780 reports speak of numerous skirmishes between smugglers and officials on Horsham Common but details are scarce. One encounter took place two years later on the 31st of May, 1782, when Horsham's Chief Revenue Officer, Thomas Walter, accompanied by some Dragoons, stumbled upon eight smugglers. After a shoot out in which one bootlegger died, five horses loaded with tea were captured.

From 1815 onwards the Government, having won the war against Napoleon, felt able to divert more resources to the fight against smugglers. From this time onwards the job of avoiding the dreaded Excisemen became harder and harder until finally smuggling was all but stamped out.

The Shipley Gang had its origins in smuggling but soon branched out to try other things. At their peek between the years 1815-18 they were involved in highway robbery, burglary, mill smashing, sheep stealing and poaching. Consisting mainly of members from the Rapleys this gang also specialised in surrounding and attacking lone farm houses in the dead of night. These attacks took place in Rowhook, Rudgwick, Billingshurst, Thakeham, Ashurst, Shermanbury, Nuthurst and Horsham.
The leader of the gang was James Rapley Senior a man known everyone by his nickname of Robin Hood. Other members were as follows:- Joseph Rapley, James Rapley junior, Daniel Rapley, Sarah Rapley, James Jupp, William Langley Senior and junior, James Evans, James Nye and William Brown. An attempt to catch the gang at a cottage at the bottom of Bonfire Hill Southwater failed but most were rounded up at another house in Itchingfield. The date was August 1818.
'Robin Hood' hanged himself whilst the rest of the gang were sentenced to death only to be reprieved and transported.

On a clear moonlit night in February, 1832, a Steyning man, William Cowerson, was shot dead whilst helping smugglers protect their contraband. The goods had just been unloaded on Worthing beach when Customs Excisemen moved in to make arrests. Cowerson attacked one official, Lt. Henderson, with a club breaking his arm. But he should have broke the other because it carried the pistol that was to end his life. Henderson fired point blank killing him almost instantly.
Cowerson's body was eventually transported to Steyning churchyard where he was laid to rest.

THE SUSSEX BOUNTY HUNTER

The Customs Excisemen were not the only ones trying to put an end to the smugglers in Sussex. John Rogers, an enthusiastic bounty hunter, was also on the job. His main problem though seemed to be that the authorities did not fully appreciate his efforts in this field. On one day in August, 1721, he captured a trafficker named Edward Tomkins at West Chiltington and turned him over to the forces of law and order. They promptly charged Rogers with making an illegal arrest and threw him into gaol. Tomkins, a member of the notorious Mayfield gang, escaped unpunished.

The powers that be also disciplined Rogers some time later after he had rounded up a group of nine smugglers. They ruled that the bootleggers could only be brought to trial if they had been caught 'in the act' as it were. They were not and Rogers was given a taste of the whip for his troubles.

TORTURE IN HORSHAM

It seems that the Assessors in old Horsham were not in possession of a great number of instruments of torture. This, no doubt, was a fact that pleased local criminals and smugglers no end.

Perhaps the authorities did not have at their fingers the money that would have enabled them to commission the building of instruments such as The Rack or The German Skull Crusher (a particularly nasty device that persuaded your lower teeth that they would be more favourably positioned if they were situated in the base of your brain).

But one thing was certain. When the men of the court wanted something bad enough they were not beyond using a little persuasion to get it. And with little in the way of instruments to hand they had to construct something that would be simple, cheap and effective. This meant execution by 'Peine forte et dure' or 'severe and hard punishment'.

This method of torture meant that the victim had to be spread-eagled out and then manacled to the floor so that they faced upwards. From then on large weights would be positioned on the chest until the victim broke down and either died or gave the gaolers the information or confession they sought. Some torturers placed a small stone directly under the back bone of the sufferer to achieve a quicker admission or to cripple them.

The last man to die in Horsham, and indeed England, from 'A Pressing' as it was known, was John Weekes, of Fittleworth. He appeared at Lewes court in August, 1735 along with three accomplices, one of which was a boy called William Steere. The group were charged with the robbery and murder of a Miss Elizabeth Symonds at her cottage in Petworth on May 14th of the same year. The gang had used the boy to climb in through a window and unlock the door thus giving the gang access to the isolated property. But they must have made some noise because Miss Symonds awoke and came down stairs to investigate the disturbance.

As she entered a downstairs room she was set upon by the robbers and cruelly murdered. Her killers then set about destroying the inside of the little cottage in search of valuables. Having found several items of interest they made their getaway and disappeared into the night.

After an exhaustive hunt the authorities found some of the stolen property, arrested the gang and managed to talk the young boy into turning King's evidence. The boy's statement convicted two of the accomplices and they were taken away and hanged, but John Weekes had other ideas.

When asked to plead he simply refused to say anything. This annoyed the judges who, after bringing in eight witnesses, all of whom swore that Weekes could in fact talk and was not dumb, gave the man a little time in the cells to rethink his strategy.

At the end of his time Weekes still refused to utter even a single word and so the Judges were forced to find the defendant not guilty of the crime of murder. Instead they convicted him of 'standing mute through malice' and read out the following sentence to him:-

' That the prisoner shall be sent to the prison from which he came, and put into a mean room stopped from the light and shall there be laid on the bare ground without any litter, straw or other covering, and without any garment about him except at his waist. He shall lie upon his back, his head shall be covered and his feet shall be bare. One of his arms shall be drawn with a cord to one side of the room and the other arm to the other side and his legs shall be served in like manner. Then shall be laid upon his body as much iron or stone as he can bear and more and the first day after he shall have three morsels of barley bread without any drink, and the second day he shall be allowed to drink as much as he can at three times of the water that is next the prison door, except running water, without any bread, and this shall be his diet till he dies. And he against whom this judgement shall be given forfeits his goods to the King.'

Weekes was returned to his original place of confinement, Horsham gaol, and readied for death. His gaolers though decided to deviate from the sentence handed down and instead of torturing Weekes in some dungeon or other, chose to press him in the prison courtyard, a place that was apparently open to the general public.

The 'Dumb Man' as he was now being called was brought from his cell and laid out in the fashion instructed. Next a large board was placed over his prostrate body and one hundredweight rested thereon. After some time during which Weekes uttered no sound a second and then a third hundredweight was added to the board. With large crowds now in attendance a further fifty pounds was positioned on the murderer causing him to writhe in the agonies of death.

At this point the gaoler, a man who supposedly weighed in the region of sixteen stone, jumped onto Weekes crushing the last drop of life from him.

The total bill for the imprisonment, transportation and execution of Weekes and his accomplices was £2. 3. 4.

Local folklore says that the death of the executioner was directly linked to his handling of Weekes's body.   The first story says that whilst he was transporting the body away to be buried in 'Hells Corner', St Mary's, it accidentally fell from its wheelbarrow at the corner outside the Kings Head Hotel. The other story says that he saw a light on in The Crown and, before popping in for drink with the pub's Porter, hid the body in a nearby passage. Either way the outcome after this unexpected stop for Weekes was to prove none to healthy for his handler. Some time later he is said to have dropped dead on the very same spot where Weekes had fallen from the barrow.

Fig. 8. The last man tortured to death in England died at Horsham.

44

THE HORSHAM HANG FAIRS

Hangings in Horsham were almost always carried out on the Common in the early days. As these events were always a public spectacle they were held on a Saturday at high noon. The Common itself no longer exists but in its day it was a striking feature of the town. Described as being a mile wide it stretched from the Brighton Road up to the then hamlet of Roughey and was a mixture of bracken, heath, and pretty windmills. It was also a place where many of those executed had committed their original crimes of robbery and assault.

Not much is known about the exact place or places where the early executions were carried out but later hangings occurred near Champion's mill, the windmill which was once located between the bridge by the railway station and the roundabout situated at the north end of King's Road.

After the County Gaol was moved from the Carfax to East Street in 1779 a new hanging site was used at the top of Hornbrook Hill. The exact location of this was around 30 yards north of the Brighton Road, almost opposite Kerves Lane at an area now covered by Sandeman Way. At the time of the hangings it became known as 'The Hanging Plat'.

As with most events, large crowds gathered on hanging days to watch the convicted criminals as they were brought from their gaol cells and taken by wagon to the gallows. The method used to hang criminals on the Common was brutally simple. They were blindfolded with a white hood and made to stand in the back of their wagon. The noose was then put about their neck, tightened, and when the time was right, the wagon was driven away allowing the villain to swing.

All bodies were left hanging for one hour before they were taken down and readied for disposal. They were either buried in the extreme south west corner of the old churchyard, buried elsewhere by their kin or between 1752 and 1832 given to local doctors for dissection. Those convicted of the most violent of crimes were enclosed in man shaped cages known as gibbets and left to rot at the scenes of their crimes.

Old records provide evidence that many criminals escaped the ultimate punishment by being transported to the colonies.

THE HANGINGS

The earliest recorded crimes punished by execution date from as far back as 1306 when eight people were found guilty of a variety of offences which included cattle theft. In those times it was not uncommon for people to be burned to death for their crimes so the hangman's rope must have been preferred by some if only for its quickness of action.

With records non-existent or in a bad state of repair reports of executions from the early centuries are hard to come by. But two hangings that happened in the sixteenth century have come to light.

On the 15th of June, 1541, Richard Sowton, from the village of Nuthurst, was hanged for the crime of coining money. Later, in 1598, a Horsham labourer named Robert Johnson swung for making two twopenny pieces out of tin.

Records from the eighteenth century are a good deal more comprehensive.

In 1734, when a Jewish pedlar by the name of Jacob Harris was found guilty of triple murder and robbery at The Royal Oak on Ditchling Common the Horsham Assessors did not hesitate to hand him down a death sentence. He was to be clamped in irons and chains and hung to death on the town's Common. A post stands in Ditchling marking the approximate spot where he was gibbeted. This pole is topped with a figure of a rooster. At the time local superstition told that if a piece of 'Jacobs post' was broken off it could be used to cure all manner of ills.

In all 43 criminals were tried and hanged on Horsham Common between the years 1735 and 1752. Of these eight were horse thieves, twelve burglars, four smugglers, two sheep stealers, six robbers and eleven murderers.

After robbing Elizabeth Swann on the highway, John Nye also found his way to Horsham's Common on the 25th of March, 1769, no doubt with the help of a large crowd and a Gaoler.

Around 1770 a post boy by the name of William Bowles, was robbed of his bag by an old man called John Upperton. On being captured Upperton denied that he had anything to do with the crime but this did not help him one little bit. Come the 6th of April Upperton was hanged and his body transported back to the scene of the crime where it was enclosed and hung in a gibbet for all to see.

On some occasions it was necessary to make multiple executions due to the fact that the Assessors had convicted so many. One such case happened on the 30th, August, 1773, when three men dropped together for a variety of crimes.

The first was William Stamp, a notorious 'road inspector' or mugger who spent many nights walking the byways around Horsham robbing travellers of their valuables. His methods were brutally simple and direct. He would spring from concealment, grab for the horse's bridle and attack his victim with a large cudgel, knocking him senseless before he knew what was happening. Once his victim was down and unconscious on the muddy track he would rifle through their belongings relieving them of any valuables such as silver or gold.

The second was a youth in his teens who went by the name of Richard Bridger. This young man had stolen one hundred pounds (a considerable sum in those days) at Chichester.

The third and last man was Ambrose Cannon, a member of a smuggling gang which had killed a soldier during a brawl at Arundel 16 years earlier in 1757. Cannon protested against his sentence saying that he had 'gone straight', got married and had lived an honest life since the murder and that these fact should have been taken into account.

A group of local gentry drew up a petition to help Cannon but later abandoned the idea much to his annoyance. His wife reportedly broke down as he was taken to the gallows and hanged along with Stamp and Bridger but the crowd felt great sympathy for her and a collection was held that raised a considerable sum.

In his diary of 1773, John Baker of Horsham Park House mentions that he saw the condemned men transported by his house between five and six in the afternoon. He confirms that the executions took place one hundred yards north of Champions, the first windmill.

The year 1776, saw Ann Cruttenden burnt at the stake and Richard Tompkyns hanged. Tompkyns had jumped ship on the Thames after being sentenced to a period of either hard labour or transportation. He was twenty five years old and left a wife and child.

William Garrett was found guilty of shooting his wife and died at the end of a rope in March, 1780. He said before his death that he regretted what he had done and had no complaints about the sentence handed down. A cell-mate of Garrett's, George Dilloway, was tried at the same court for manslaughter and sent to a Man-of-War but he 'was discharged by proclamation' after he cut off the first and forth fingers of his right hand with a knife.

The 25th, August, 1783, saw Thomas Jones, Robert Parsons and John Beach hanged on the Common for robbery. As these men walked from the prison they each gave a polite bow to the Sheriff before going to their doom. The hanging itself was bungled as the executioner had to spend several minutes pulling on the legs of the men to bring about death.

Nine months later on the 14th, April, 1784, William Darby and Joseph Varnfield were executed before the usual large crowd. Varnfield, a burglar, was very vocal from the moment he knew his fate. On being taken from the East Grinstead court he cried, 'make way for a dead man,' and just before his death he said, 'he feared not death but would have liked to have met it at the hands of a man.' He went on to say, 'that his executioner didn't look like one.'

1785, saw Benjamin Kennard, 23, hanged for stealing five pounds worth of goods. He is said to have met his death with courage and fortitude and left behind him a wife and two children. Also that same year, John Carpenter, a hardened criminal, met his end bravely in Horsham. He had been moved down from Newgate Prison and convicted at Lewes before finally arriving at the Common. Accounts of his hanging say that the noose placed about his neck was positioned wrongly which caused him to, 'struggle long and hard with his fate'. His executioner was showered with rocks after his bad job and forced to leave the Common in a hurry.

On April the 8th, 1786, William Hartly, Joseph Clark and William Edwards were all hanged together for burglary, robbery, and highway robbery. Later in August John Wells and Thomas Paine were also done away with.

Richard Scipio Bristow robbed Mr. Hards at gun point of two and a half guineas and a pint of beer on Staplefield Common, 19th, December, 1786. He was captured at Copthorne and eventually hanged at

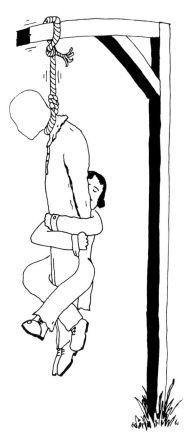

Fig. 9. Robert Parsons is helped on his way by Horsham's hangman, 1783.

Horsham. Two other men, John Wilder, 21, and Charles Roberts, 40, died with him. Not much is known about Roberts except that he was a Frenchman. It seems this fact alone may have been a good enough reason to kill him.

In 1788, William Sill was sentenced to hang for the crime of horse theft. As Sill rode in the wagon with his coffin it was noticed that his hangman was blind drunk. Several times during the walk up the Brighton Road he was forced to take a grip on the condemned man's cart in order to steady himself. During the hanging itself he only remained upright by using the horse thief as support. In the end he succeeded in hanging the man much to the surprise of the watching crowd.

Only one man was hanged in 1789, and his name was James Winn. He was convicted at East Grinstead of stealing a horse from Mr. Walter, a well known Customs Officer at Horsham.

1790 saw the death of eight men on the Common. The first of these was Richard Grazemark who was found guilty of murdering his daughter. He had also attempted the murder of his son-in-law. After wishing everyone well and telling them that he meant no harm he dropped to his death from the back of his cart. After he had 'twisted' for the customary one hour his body was cut down and sold to two Horsham surgeons, Price and Popay. These men then gave a public exhibition of their skills which involved removing the dead man's skin so that it could be given to a tanner and turned into leather. Several local people put their names down for a piece of this gruesome material. After the skinning had taken place the body was dissected and the bones boiled.

Fig. 10. Doctors boil the bones of Richard Grazemark on Horsham Common, 1790.

Cooper Goodsiff, George Summers and John Saunders were executed a few months later for involvement in horse theft and burglary. Goodsiff's wife walked eighty miles to see her husband off. Their last farewells were by all account very moving. The following Saturday a highwayman, Philip Davey, and three horse thieves, William Brook, James West and Thomas Smith all met their maker before a large mob on Horsham Common.

Three soldiers found their way to the gallows in 1795, for stealing 50 bushels of flour and the serious crime of mutiny. William Sykes and William Sanson were hanged on the 13th of June whilst William Midwinter felt the rope on the 8th of August. Reports at the time say a large collection was made for one of the soldier's widows.

Thomas Hilton, 18, died on the 4th of August, 1795, for the crime of highway robbery.

1799 saw two mail robbers, Robert and William Drewett, hanged on the Common for a crime committed at North Heath, an area near to their home town of Midhurst. Robert apparently kept silent before his death but William shouted at the crowd that he was innocent of the crime. After the hanging the bodies were returned to the gaol, placed in irons and taken to the scene of their crime. At Petworth the crowd was so big that the officials could not pass through the town and had to lock the men's bodies up for a time. The brothers were eventually gibbeted on a post that was 32 feet high.

A woman, Edith Lavendar, swung in 1799, for the killing of her unwanted child. Aged only seventeen she is said to have, 'trembled and wept much,' before her death.

In March of 1801 two gentlemen horse thieves were sentenced to hang for stealing two racing fillies, 'Miscreant' and 'Duchess of Limbs'. William and James Card continued to act in a superior and snooty fashion until they took the drop on the 11th of August. They were buried in the south west corner of the old Horsham churchyard along with others who had been put to death down the years.

Later, on the 11th of August, James Gaston followed them to their resting place for the same crime of horse theft.

1802 saw the execution of two related men who shared the surname of Beatson. Convicted of stealing £3500 at Wall Hill, Forest Row, they were brought down from Bow Street, London, and hanged at Horsham.

1803 saw Robert Bignell charged with the murder of smuggler named Webber. Acting as he was, as an informer for the authorities, Bignell was acquitted of the crime and left Sussex for Bristol. Whilst away he carried on working for Customs Excise as a stool pigeon but when he felt the need for a little extra money he wouldn't hesitate to go out and rob people for it.

Later he returned south and after being convicted of a felony charge found himself incarcerated within the walls of Rochester gaol. From here he made a daring escape with another prisoner named Tingley. Both men subsequently robbed a house in Albourne but were foolish enough to leave the cover of the forest and go to Ditchling where the Landlord of the White Hart Inn recognised Bignell. The year was now 1807.

After being captured and paraded in court Tingley was acquitted. Bignell again tried to escape but he suffered a severe attack of cramp and fell from the ladder he was scaling. He was then sent to Horsham to be hanged for his crimes. In gaol he turned to poetry and religion to such a degree that on the day of his hanging he even joined in with the chaplain as prayers were read on his behalf. After being allowed to read some of his own poetry, the theme of which was evil, he was hanged before a crowd 3000 strong. The events of this day were well remembered by Horsham folk for many years. It was not uncommon to hear someone remark, 'oh, that was around the time old Bignell was hung, wasn't it?' or, 'Yes, I remember little Johnny being born. He came into the world about the same time Bignell left it, didn't he?'

After Bignell's hanging it was rumoured that his ill gotten gains, some £400, was to be recovered by a fellow prisoner and split with his wife. During Bignell's escapades, in the year 1805, it is recorded that a further six people were hanged in the town. George Williams, 28, for stealing three saddles and bridles, William King, 64, for sheep stealing, William Harris for burglary and Ann Davis for killing her unwanted baby. Later in August the last two, Josiah Groombridge and William Boon swung for the same crime as King, sheep theft.

1807 saw one Edward Ball, a cultured man of 35 years, hanged for forging a £5 note.

Two years later a 27 year old man named William Turner was executed for the theft of £90 and two watches.

When William Treble was sentenced to be hanged along with William Wilson and William Langley no one guessed that he would never make it to the official gallows. Shortly before he was to die, the forger took his own life by hanging himself from the bars across his cell window. His body was buried at the cross-roads on the Common. 400 people watched Wilson and Langley hang. The year was 1810.

Records show that between 1810 and 1818 there were many more transportations than hangings. From this time on executions became less frequent until they were done away with altogether.

1817 was an unlucky year for a man named Falconer. He was one of sixteen men sentenced to be executed but in the end the only one actually hanged as the rest were sent abroad.

In 1819 James Gibbs was hanged after he attempted to murder someone at Storrington.

The 11th of August saw Edward Broadbent, a private in the 90th Foot, executed after he shot to death a bullying sergeant. By all reports this execution was one of the worst ever carried out in Horsham. The hangman, who was new to the job and inexperienced at rope craft prepared the cord to the wrong length and as a result Private Broadbent's feet touched the ground as he fell from the wagon. The poor wretch was finally killed after several officials dug a small hole under his feet which allowed him to 'hang properly'.

Learning from his mistakes the hangman it seems had no trouble dispatching two more villains later that month. A burglar, John Piper, and a sheep stealer, John Lulham, were the last to die that year. Before he died, Piper, a man not at all happy with his predicament, shouted at those before him. 'Why is it only the poor who are hanged? The laws of England are fine for stringing up a man like a dog.' He also added, 'a poor man, if he has no rich friends, is bound to suffer gratitude.' After they had hung for the required hour, friends claimed the bodies so that they might be buried in their home parishes. A crowd of 2000 saw them off.

One year later horse thief Daniel Hartford became the last man to be hanged on the Common. Not many people turned out for the execution because word had it that he would not be 'done' by the new device called the Newgate drop. Many people wanted to see this new method of dispatching crooks. The Newgate drop was in fact a portable hanging station that could easily be erected anywhere and was strong enough to carry the weight of an entire execution party.

This new device was finally pressed into service on the 24th of August 1822 when Henry Durrant and James Tilley were sentenced to swing for carrying out an aggravated burglary. Later that same week Davis Barnett shared the same fate having committed the same crime.

1826 saw the wrongful execution of a young boy who went by the name of Leney. Convicted on circumstantial evidence he and Hannah Russell were sentenced to death for the murder of the woman's husband. Protesting his innocence to the last the boy was hanged to death without mercy.

Hannah Russell had more luck though when her lawyer succeeded in delaying her execution by means of a petition. During the following year it was discovered that her husband had died from natural causes and she was released from gaol.

The following year saw William Burt hanged for the murder of his own child, committed it is said, in a fit of drunken rage.

Another William, this time with the surname Holloway, died in 1831 after he did away with his wife.

In the winter of 1830 large disturbances occurred throughout the countryside on account of low pay. Many farm labourers took up arms and marched to the doors of their employers demanding a fair day's pay for a fair day's work.

Not satisfied with some of the answers they got they forced some to accompany them on a march into the town where a meeting was to be held. The end result of the meeting was that landowners and farmers agreed to raise wages to at least 2 shillings for a day's work. After the march a body of soldiers was sent to be stationed at Horsham under the command of Col. Fludyer and Capt. Gore.

A nasty side effect of the troubles was an activity known as rick firing. Subversive elements would deliberately set fire to corn stacks to cause their employers substantial losses. Between 1830 and 1834 five men were convicted of this crime and hanged for it. Their names were as follows:- Edmund Bushby, Thomas Bufford, Samuel Thorncraft, George Wren and William Goodsell. Of these men executed, the case of the young George Wren was the most controversial as the evidence against him was extremely flimsy.

When the fire he was accused of starting first broke out Wren was known to have been in his work house. No one saw him at the scene before the blaze started and after the alarm was raised he even helped tackle the fire by throwing buckets of water on it. Wren was convicted after his boot prints were found at the scene of the burning. To make matters worse for poor Wren the judge raised the lad's hopes by delaying his death. But in the end it came to nothing.

Records show that public sympathy was on the side of the condemned 17 year old as he was led from his cell and up onto the gallows in East Street. A huge crowd had gathered not to see him swing but to see him get off. And indeed an eyewitness said at the time that the mood of the mob was such that if anyone had spoken up and demanded the boy's release he would have had the whole of the town behind him in an instant. But no one had courage enough to do so.

Wren protested his innocence from the top of the wooden gallows and named several who had given false evidence against him to no avail.

He was hanged by the neck until dead.

As his body twisted in the wind a small robin redbreast was seen to settle on his shoulder. Someone shooed it away but it returned, and to many in the crowd this was proof positive that the boy was as innocent as he had said he was. Some years later a carrier gave a death-bed confession in which he admitted setting fire to the rick. He had also stolen the boy's boots so as to leave Wren's footprints at the scene.

Another of those hanged, William Goodsell, had a long criminal history with involvement in up to sixteen robberies. His mother, who owned a beer shop, had directed him in all of his crimes.

Richard Sheppard, an ex footman and burglar was the last man to escape from the Horsham gaol but it did him no good. He was soon caught and in 1835 hanged along with John Sparshatt.

In 1837, an act of Parliament changed the law so that only those found guilty of treason and murder could be hanged.

A STRANGE THING TO DO WITH THE DEAD

People in old Horsham were superstitious when it came to most things and that included those recently hanged. Women with skin complaints believed that they could be cured if they were to come into contact with the dead.

As the corpses dangled limply from the gallows these women would slip the executioner a few pennies in order that they might have their necks touched by the hands of the recently departed.

THE LAST EXECUTION IN HORSHAM

This took place on Saturday the 6th of April, 1844, the day of the Teg Fair in Horsham. The man convicted of murder and sentenced to die was John Lawrence of Tunbridge Wells. Coming from a respectable family Lawrence had fallen in with a bad crowd after throwing away the chance of a steady job arranged by his father. Feeling restless he upped sticks and moved to the seaside town of Brighton. Here it is said he made his mark on the town's underworld by, among other things, ruthlessly kicking a woman who tried to stop him stealing her jewellery.

In March of 1844 he was arrested for stealing a roll of carpet from a shop in St. James Street, Brighton, and escorted to the Police station. After being interviewed about the crime Lawrence dashed to a fireplace, grabbed a poker and hit Superintendent Solomon viciously about the head causing his death. With three people having witnessed the murder Lawrence was convicted without leaving the dock and was ordered to be taken straight to the condemned cell at Horsham.

On the day of his execution fully 3000 people massed in the town to watch the spectacle and enjoy the fair. Amongst them was Lawrence's brother, a man who confessed to being drunk and admitted to being a greater scoundrel than his brother although he had never committed murder.

As the gallows, painted black and covered in parts by canvas, towered up above the crowd so pedlars walked around selling copies of so called dying confessions. A notorious beer seller named old Whiting, whose shop was almost opposite the gaol, did a roaring trade by all accounts. This man was well known in the town for keeping a rough house much frequented by beggars, gamblers and troublemakers.

When the time came the crowd gathered around the place of execution. This was located on the west front of the Gaol which is an area just east of where the railway bridge in East Street is now. The gallows themselves are described as being on the north side of the road and facing towards Denne Park. With a large body of London Police on duty outside the prison, Lawrence was escorted out at 12 o'clock noon and walked up onto the structure of death. A hush fell over the expectant crowd.

As the chaplain spoke the last words John Lawrence was ever to hear, a white hood was placed over the condemned man's head. Next came the noose and before the chaplain had finished speaking Lawrence dropped to his death.

His body was buried within the gaol around the site of the old chapel in Park Terrace East but later exhumed when the prison was pulled down. Before being re-buried in the south west corner of the churchyard the body of John Lawrence was kept for a short time in the stables at the Queen's Head Public House. Anyone who wanted to view the gruesome remains could do so for a small charge of 2d.

BURNED AT THE STAKE IN HORSHAM

Ann Whale was born unto the respected Waterton family in 1731. Her father, the Landlord of the Cock Inn, sited in the Carfax, died while she was young and by all accounts she fell in with bad company. After many arguments with her mother she left this group and came back into the family fold where she was quickly matched with a reliable labouring man. They were married soon after in 1749.

The happy couple then spent time living in West Chiltington and Pulborough before having their first child and moving to Broadbridge Heath. Here they lived in a house known as Corsletts that was owned at the time by Mr John Agate. Another part of the house was occupied by Ann's older cousin, Sarah Pledge, her seven children and husband James.

Around this time Ann learned that she was to receive £80 from the will of a dead uncle and this seems to have played on the mind of Sarah who attempted to worm her way into a position whereas she could get her hands on at least some of the money. This annoyed the husband of Anne who forbade Sarah from entering his side of the house.

Some time after this episode one of the women suggested that James Whale should be done away with. The statements made by the women at the time indicate that both blamed each other for making this suggestion and later plotting the murder.

Ann Whale accuses Sarah of attempting to buy poison in Dorking and Rusper and of putting spiders in a bottle of beer belonging to James. The statement of Sarah Pledge says that Ann offered her half a guinea to buy a new dress if she would obtain some poison for her.

It also appears that Sarah's husband offered at one time to purchase the toxin but he withdrew his offer soon after. In the end Sarah Pledge went to Horsham and brought one pennyworth of a substance known as White Mercury (a kind of Arsenic) from a Mr. Harfey.

On the 9th of October, James Whale sat down to lunch and ate a pudding containing the deadly powder. One half hour later he began to feel very ill but continued as best he could with his work despite appalling stomach aches and severe bouts of vomiting. During the night he suffered horribly before eventually dying at seven o'clock the next morning.

At his inquest four people gave evidence that Whale's body bore no traces of violence and it was decided that a 'visitation of Almighty God' had been the cause of the man's death. But a chance conversation proved the undoing of the women who believed they had got away with murder.

When James Agate entered the shop where Sarah Pledge had brought the poison he was surprised when Mr. Harfey asked him if he had, 'got rid of his rats yet?'

Mr. Agate replied that he had no rats and in the discussion that followed he learnt of the recently purchased poison. His suspicions aroused he asked a few questions which had the effect of starting a new inquiry into the fate of James Whale.

Ann Whale along with Sarah and James Pledge were eventually arrested and charged with murder. During the proceedings James Pledge was discharged by Proclamation but the two women faired much worse. Sarah was found guilty of being an accessory and sentenced to hang whilst her partner in crime was told she would be burnt at the stake. In prison both women are said to have fallen out but as the time of their execution neared they apparently reconciled after receiving the last sacrament.

At 3.30pm on the 7th of August, 1752, Sarah Pledge was hanged on Broadbridge Heath Common. After the executioner had taken her clothes (which was his right under custom) her body was transported to Storrington and dissected by local doctors. It is recorded that this was the first example of this kind of analysis to occur in Sussex.

Two hours later at 5.30pm before a crowd so big it had to be seen to be believed, Ann Whale was tied to a stake and fired. Her body was reduced to ashes in a matter of five minutes and her screams heard as far away as Cindermill Farm, Warnham.

Twenty six years later in 1776, another Ann, this time with the surname Cruttenden, was put to death for murder and mutilation. Aged in her late 70s, she was married to a Brightling butcher who was half her age. Not surprisingly the relationship between the two was not good and she eventually killed and butchered the body of her husband. Some observers at the time believed the old woman's behaviour in prison showed her to be quite clearly mad but these were hard times and she was sentenced to burn. On the 8th of August, 1776, she was transported by wagon to Horsham Common and, at a few minutes past midday, burned to death at the stake.

Fig. 11. Ann Whale was burned to death in Broadbridge Heath for the crime of murder, 1752.